You Can Pull Down Strongholds And Break Old Habits

You Can Pull Down Strongholds And Break Old Habits

Casey Treat

You Can Do It!

ISBN 1-57921-070-6
LCCN 97-62079

Published by Christian Faith International
PO Box 98800
Seattle, WA 98198

Contents

Introduction

When a person is first born again and becomes a new creature in Christ Jesus, their thoughts, words, and actions are fortified with the world's philosophies, deceits, and traditions. Paul warns us in Colossians 2:8: *Beware lest anyone cheat you through philosophy and empty deceit, according to the tradition of men, according to the basic principles of the world, and not according to Christ.*

In Romans 12:2 Paul said, *And do not be conformed to this world, but be transformed by the renewing of your mind.*

When you are born again, your *spirit* is instantly changed. The *body* is not changed, but will be saved when the Lord returns. At that time the corruptible will put on incorruption and the mortal will put on immortality (see 1 Corinthians 15:52-54). The *soul*—made up of the mind, will, and emotions—is the part of man that we are to take charge of and feed with God's Word, bringing it in line with the Word. It is not "saved" when we are born again, but it is "being saved" as we feed it spiritually.

Many Christians do not experience God's will because they are not in the process of transformation. They have been trained to hang on until Jesus comes, or to accept the way things are "because God is teaching me something through my circumstances."

As we begin to renew our minds with God's Word, we will begin to establish the perfect will of God on the earth *now* rather than when we get to the "sweet by and by." We'll no longer put up with the "rotten here and now." We'll change it by pulling down Satan's lies and deceptions with God's Word of truth.

The "how to's" of pulling down strongholds, breaking old habits, and transforming your mind to think and speak and act as God thinks, speaks, and acts are learned as you saturate yourself daily with God's Word.

Throughout this teaching, *Renewal Truths* have been prepared in personal confession form and are highlighted, which, if believed and acted upon, will put you "in step" with God's perfect will—His destiny—for your life. The "Personal Application of Renewal Truths" at the end of each chapter will also help to reinforce this teaching.

CASEY TREAT

1

Setting Your Mind on God's Word

A s a born-again believer, you can only become all God has designed you to be as you are *renewed in the knowledge of God*. Maturity, success, and enjoyment as a Christian will only come as you are renewed in knowledge after the image of the One who created you.

When you are born again, positionally you become a new person. Then you must set your mind on things above—on the principles of God found in His Word, His way of thinking. Setting your mind on things above does not mean that you should walk around thinking about heaven all day long. First of all, we don't know that much about heaven. We would be speculating and making things up. If God wanted us to know more about heaven, He would have told us more. He wants us to set our minds on the principles, on the way of thinking, and on the spiritual thoughts that come from heaven.

We fail to become successful, fulfilled, and overcoming Christians if our minds have not been renewed in the knowledge of God. We fail to take off the old man—the old habits of our carnal nature and put away that old lifestyle—and put on the new man, who is created in the image and likeness of God, if our minds are not renewed with the promises of God's Word.

In Colossians, chapter 3, Paul talks about setting our minds on "things above" once we are born again:

> *If then you were raised with Christ* [if you are born again, if your name is written in the Lamb's Book of Life], *seek those things which are above, where Christ is, sitting at the right hand of God. Set your mind on things above, not on things on the earth. For you died, and your life is hidden with Christ in God.*
>
> Colossians 3:1–3

Paul is saying, "If you are born again, the next step is to set your mind in the right place." If you are risen with Christ, seek those things which are above and set your mind on them—not on the things of the earth.

> *When Christ who is our life appears, then you also will appear with Him in glory. Therefore* [because you are a Christian and you are "in Christ"] *put to death your members which are on the earth: fornication, uncleanness, passion, evil desire, and covetousness, which is idolatry. Because of these things the wrath of God is coming upon the sons of disobedience, in which you yourselves once walked when you lived in them. But now you yourselves are to put off all these: anger, wrath, malice, blasphemy, filthy language out of your mouth. Do not lie to one another, since you have put off the old man with his deeds, and have put on the new man who is renewed in knowledge according to the image of Him who created him, where there is neither Greek nor Jew, circumcised nor uncircumcised, barbarian, Scythian, slave nor free, but Christ is all and in all.*
>
> Verses 4–11

Once you are born of God, the knowledge that you live by (or where you set your mind) is the key to every aspect of your life. As a Christian, the success or failure, fulfillment or lack of fulfillment, enjoyment or lack of enjoyment, blessing or lack of blessing you experience, is dependent upon *where you set your mind*—whether you are renewed in the knowledge of God or not.

Renewal Truth

The Word of Christ dwells in me richly in all wisdom.
(Colossians 3:16)

GOD GAVE MAN THE POWER OF CHOICE

God created man with a sovereign will and with the ability to think through the processes of life. If we don't use our will and our mental ability properly, we will not rise to the level of life that God created for us to enjoy. God will not determine our will or use our mental ability for us. He created us in His likeness and image, with a freedom to make choices.

If you were a monkey, He would have programmed you internally to do what He wanted you to do. He would have put within you the instincts that would control your life, and you wouldn't have any choices to make. If you were a dog, God would have programmed you to do what He wanted you to do. If you were a bird, when the right time came, you would head south whether you ever thought about it or not. But, the good news is, you are not an animal!

No matter how hard scientists work to prove that we are part of the animal kingdom, they will never find the missing link. We were created in the likeness and image of God, with an open mind, the ability to choose, and the ability to think. We must use these rights biblically, or we will not find our place in God where our life will satisfy and fulfill us. Instead, we will struggle and keep on struggling and never find our place of fulfillment.

CHOOSE LIFE!

Deuteronomy 30:19 says:

I call heaven and earth as witnesses today against you, that I have set before you life and death, blessing and cursing; therefore choose life, that both you and your descendants may live.

The Bible says that when we stand before God—either after death or after the rapture of the Church—we will give an account of our lives. We cannot give an account for something that we were not in charge of or that we did not have control over. We will give an account of our lives, which is a summation of the choices we made. To say that we were a victim, or that what we did was not our fault, is to deny the reality of the Word of God. God sets before us life and death and He says, *"Choose life."*

As a young man who had already messed things up, who had created all kinds of problems for myself and the people around me, who was discouraged and depressed about life in general, when someone said, "God has given you an opportunity to change," that excited me.

"You mean I can do something about my life?" Yes! "You mean my life doesn't have to be like this?" No! "You mean I'm not just set on a course called 'fate'?" No! There is no such thing as fate. You don't have to accept anything you don't want to accept.

I got motivated—fired up! Within a few short years I turned things around in my life because of learning this truth. God created me in His image and likeness, and He gave me the power of choice.

Renewal Truth

Because I am created in the image and likeness of God, I have the power to *choose life*. I choose life!
(Genesis 1:26; Deuteronomy 30:19)

Now, more than twenty years later, I'm still looking for areas in my life where I can make changes. I'm looking for a mountain to which I will say, "I'll climb you." I'm looking at aspects of my life where I can say, "I'll take charge of you. I'll discipline you. I'll overcome that limitation. I'll turn that negative habit around. I will deal with that circumstance." Where you set your mind will control how you live your life. I am continually looking for areas where the choices I make will set the course of my life and put me on the path God has set for me.

The heart is made up of the spirit and the soul, which is actually the spiritual womb of your life. Out of it you give birth to all the good things and the bad things that happen in your life.

Sometimes we like to *mystify* or *spiritualize* biblical teachings to the point where we don't feel responsible for them because we don't really understand them. For example, after a sermon, some-one says, "Wasn't that great?" to which another person responds, "Yeah, but what did he say?" "I don't know, but it was really good!"

Since it was so cool, so deep, you feel blessed, but you didn't *change* anything. That's why we like to talk about the Antichrist, the rapture, and the tribulation. They are really cool and spiritual, but you don't have to *do* anything. However, when you study the Word, *it's not that mystical, nor is it that deep.* It is very practical.

MAN IS KNOWN BY HIS FRUIT

In Matthew 12:33 Jesus says, *Either make the tree good and its fruit good, or else make the tree bad and its fruit bad; for a tree is known by its fruit.* You can't change the fruit on a tree. An apple tree can't bear pears and pear trees can't bear peaches, but you *can* change the fruit in *your* life.

Renewal Truth

I choose to bear good fruit
for God's Kingdom.
(John 15:8)

Jesus used the tree to describe human life. *Unlike people, plants and animals can't change.* They can't renew their minds. They are born with instincts, and they live by instincts. They can't turn that around. People keep trying to keep lions in their houses like kit-ties. When the lion eats their child, they say, "How could that have happened?" You can't renew the mind of an animal.

Remember the story of the farmer who tried to make a pig his indoor pet? As soon as the pig had a chance, he was right back in the mud. No matter how pretty he is or how clean a pig is, he is still a pig. As soon as he has a chance, he goes right back to the pigsty.

And so it is that you can't change what has been bred into the natural world. You can't change the fruit of the tree. However, you can change the fruit of your life. So Jesus says to make the tree good and its fruit good, or make the tree bad and its fruit bad. You make the choice. It's up to you. It is *your* decision. Set your mind where you want it, and it will decide the kind of life you lead, but the tree (your life) will be known by its fruit.

In our modern motivational mentality, our secular perspective of things, we don't read, "Make the tree good and its fruit good." We read, "Make the *fruit* good." We want to skip the "tree" part and get to the "fruit." We don't want to work on ourselves; we just want the benefits. So when we advertise how to be successful, how to achieve in life, or how to get out of debt, we simply advertise the benefits. No one advertises the discipline, the renewing of the mind, or the working out of this process.

• Jesus didn't say to go after the fruit. He said to change the tree, then good fruit would be automatic. Make the tree good. Get your mind right. Get your soul right. Get your spirit right. Get your heart right. Then the fruit will be right.

In Matthew 12:34, Jesus says, *Brood of vipers! How can you, being evil, speak good things? For out of the abundance of the heart the mouth speaks.*

Notice, the condition of the fruit of your life is dependent on what's going on in your heart, and what is going on in your heart is coming out of your mouth. If your heart is good, then good will

15

come out of your mouth. The Lord is trying to get us to understand—*the right heart produces the right fruit.*

Then He sums it up in verse 35: *A good man out of the good treasure of his heart brings forth good things, and an evil man out of the evil treasure brings forth evil things.* So whatever is coming out of your mouth—good or bad, rich or poor, happy or sad, big or small—is coming out of your heart.

• Many have been programmed to wait for circumstances to change so they can be happy. That's the "victim mentality." The victim says, "When everybody else changes, I'll be happy." But everybody could change and you still wouldn't be happy. The victim never changes, because he or she thinks the problem is "out there somewhere," beyond themselves, when, in fact, it's the heart that is the issue. Jesus says when you *change in your heart*, you will change the fruit of your life. Please understand, this is not to condemn but to set you free through the truth of God's Word.

Renewal Truth

Create in me a clean
heart, O God.
(Psalm 51:10)

Hebrews 4:12 says:

For the word of God is living and powerful, and sharper than any two-edged sword, piercing even to the division of soul and spirit, and of joints and marrow, and is a discerner of the thoughts and intents of the heart.

What do the *soul and spirit* do? How do they work? What are their roles? The soul includes the mind, will, and emotions. It's a connector or a joint between the spirit of man and the natural world. Everything that comes to your spirit has to get in your head or you can't use it, say it, practice it, or do anything with it. This is dangerous, because any time you get something in your spirit, you have to run it through your mind. If your mind isn't right, you will twist it. We hear a clear word from God, but by the time we interpret it, we can make it into anything we want to hear. So the connection has to be good. The soul has to be right.

Marrow is where the body creates blood. You've heard of people needing a bone marrow transplant because of a blood disease, cancer, or some other problem. The marrow is a producer or a life force. It's where the blood is created, and the blood is the life of the body.

THE THOUGHTS AND INTENTS OF THE HEART

Thoughts are the basic elements in your soul, and the intents are the basic elements of your spirit. So we've got soul and spirit, joints and marrow, and thoughts and intents. All of these are of the heart. If we get our spirit and soul, joints and marrow, and the thoughts and intents right by the Word of God, then we are going to have a good heart.

Remember Jesus' words from Matthew 12:34–35: . . . *out of the abundance of the heart the mouth speaks. A good man out of the good treasure of his heart brings forth good things, and an evil man out of the evil treasure brings forth evil things.*

If your heart has a poor connection, wrong thoughts, or anything else that's not right, then you will struggle. You won't make it. You won't get the fruit that you are looking, praying, and working for. The tree won't produce good because the heart is the key issue.

God's Word is the key to getting your heart right. The Word of God is the surgeon's scalpel of the heart. The Word of God is the sharp, two-edged sword that cuts out the stuff you don't want, sharpens the things you do want, and helps the heart to be right. The Word works in the heart, and that goes along with Mark, chapter 4, where the sower sows the Word. Where did he sow it? In the heart. So when the heart is right, your life will produce good; and when your heart isn't right, your life will be a struggle.

Now when you become a Christian, your spirit is born again. Your spirit is recreated. You become a new creature in Christ. You are one with the Spirit of God. He that is joined to the Lord is one spirit with Him. But Paul says the mind needs some work done on it.

Renewal Truth

I am a new creature in Christ Jesus. Old things have passed away, and the new has come.
(2 Corinthians 5:17)

I wish we could get the mind born again and changed instantly. "Just do it, Lord! Go ahead, I give You permission." But the Lord says, "You are made like Me, so I can't change your soul. I can recreate your spirit, but I can't change your soul. You have to do that."

So how do we do it? Go back to Colossians 3:2, *Set your mind on things above.* Then, be *renewed in knowledge according to the image of* [Jesus] (v. 10). Begin to set your mind on the right things.

Begin to change the way you think so you can think like Jesus thinks.

In every circumstance of life, I ask myself: "What would Jesus think about this? How would He respond to this? Am I being renewed in knowledge after the image of the One who created me?"

This is why it is so important that we know the Word. I don't want to make up my own interpretation of what Jesus would do. I want to base my thinking on the Word of God. That's how we learn what Jesus would do. Jesus is the Word made flesh. If you know the Word, you will know the Lord. If you don't know the Word, you won't know the Lord.

Many people ask themselves, "What would Jesus do?" If you don't know the Word, you won't have a clue. You can't be renewed in knowledge after the image of Jesus if you don't know Him. You know Jesus when you know the Word (John 1:1–4). You've got to get the Word working in your heart. <u>Set your mind on things above and be renewed in knowledge.</u> This is what Christian growth is all about.

You would think this would be an easily understood and well-known truth, but it isn't. As our television program goes out across the world, the most common response we get to this teaching is, "We've never heard this before." Now, maybe what they are saying is, their pastor taught it, they heard about it, but it never became clear to them.

We all know people who have never understood what it is to get their heart right and get their mind renewed so they can be the people God created them to be. Do you know people who just don't get it? They are waiting on the sovereign will of God. They are wondering why God allowed this or that. The truth is, what is in their life came out of their heart, but they can't see it. They can't grasp it because they have never understood that out of the heart comes our way of thinking, our way of speaking, and the fruit of our life. What is in you comes out of your mouth.

Renewal Truth

I receive the abundant life
that Jesus has come to give me,
and I reject the stealing,
killing, and destroying which
the devil has been sent to do.
I am a child of God, and His
blessings are overtaking me.
(John 10:10)

Another example of the power of the human heart is seen when we are in emergency circumstances. Studies have been done of people's responses in life and death situations. You would think that people in a life and death situation would call out to God: "Lord, forgive me. I should have gotten saved a long time ago. I'm sorry I didn't. I am giving You my life right now." But they don't.

When people are afraid, when they panic, or when they are in a life and death situation, whatever is in their heart will come out. Usually, if they are of the world, it's cursing, anger, and bitterness. For the Christian, it's praise, prayer, and faith. You can't wait until the end of your life to get right. You've got to work on your heart day by day, because at the end, whatever is in you will control you. Out of the abundance of your heart you will speak.

It may be good to give ourselves a little grace when anger, frustration, or something comes out wrong, yet it is time we take responsibility for what is coming out of the mouth. We need to realize, "If it wasn't in me, it wouldn't be coming out of me."

I'm not talking about covering it up, learning how to control your tongue, and learning how to stuff it down deeper. Your reality should be that it can't come out because it's not in your heart. You have to take responsibility to get your heart right, because out of the abundance of the heart the mouth speaks.

Most people make a good confession when they think about it: "I believe I am healed. I believe all of my needs are met. God is prospering my business. God is blessing me. My steps are ordered of the Lord." But when they are in a casual conversation with someone, they say, "I don't know what I'm going to do. We are going broke. My back is killing me."

Renewal Truth

Death and life are in the
power of my tongue. I will
speak life.
(Proverbs 18:21)

When you think about it, you make a good confession, but when you're not thinking about it, all that negative stuff in your heart comes out. That is what is killing you, keeping the pain in you, frustrating you, and keeping the curse on your life. Each of us must become responsible for the condition of our hearts and make sure that the only thing that comes out is "good" fruit.

Personal Application of
Renewal Truths

1. I set my mind on "things above" by: _____

    _____

    _____

    _____

2. I put off the old man and his evil deeds and put on the new
    man by (see Colossians 3:10): _____

    _____

    _____

    _____

    _____

3. Unlike animals, God created man with the ability to make
    choices. According to Deuteronomy 30:19, God has set
    before me life and death, blessing and cursing. Then He
    says, "_____." I choose life!

4. Good fruit will be produced in my life by: _____

    _____

    _____

    _____

    _____

5. To me, a "victim mentality" means: _____

    _____

    _____

    _____

6. My soul is made up of:
   a. _____
   b. _____
   c. _____

7. I am removing the "negatives" out of my heart and mind, and I am replacing them with "positives" that agree with God's Word by (3 examples):_____

   _____

   _____

   _____

   _____

   _____

   _____

2

The Condition of the Heart

L et's look at Matthew 15:2 the Pharisees asked Jesus, *Why do Your disciples transgress the tradition of the elders? For they do not wash their hands when they eat bread.*

That ticked Jesus off! He began to confront them and ended up calling them "hypocrites." I mean, He really dealt with them. Finally Jesus said to them, *Not what goes into the mouth defiles a man; but what comes out of the mouth, this defiles a man* (v. 11). The disciples said to Jesus, "Do You know that the Pharisees were offended by Your message today?" (v. 12). Then, in verse 15, Peter said to Jesus, *Explain this parable to us.* Jesus responded:

> *Are you also still without understanding? Do you not yet understand that whatever enters the mouth goes into the stomach and is eliminated? But those things which proceed out of the mouth come from the heart, and they defile a man. For out of the heart proceed evil thoughts.*
>
> Matthew 15:16–19

Notice, the first thing that can defile your life and that comes out of your heart is *thoughts*. Some of us have been taught that the heart is synonymous with spirit and it is separate from your mind or soul. But here we recognize what's going on in your thinking is an integral part of what is going on in your heart. I am convinced from Scripture that your heart is made up of *spirit* and *soul*. The inner man is your heart, spirit, and soul, and your heart includes your thoughts. If your thoughts aren't right, your heart isn't right.

Have you ever heard someone say, "He has a good heart but a bad temper"? In reality, although we know what is being said, it can't be so, because if you have bad thoughts, they are coming out of your heart and they can defile you.

> *For out of the heart proceed evil thoughts, murders, adulteries, fornications, thefts, false witness, blasphemies. These are the things which defile a man, but to eat with unwashed hands does not defile a man.*
>
> Matthew 15:19–20

Religion, tradition, and the world will get you to focus on all the wrong things. They will cause you to be concerned with things such as the kind of car the preacher drives, or who is serving communion, rather than the condition of the hearts of those receiving communion. All the things that God does not care about, religion gets people to focus on.

God cares about the condition of the heart, because that is where the fruit and the productivity of your life will originate. What goes on in the heart of man is relevant, because out of it springs the "quality" of life. A "right" heart will attract God's best to you, while a wrong heart will attract trouble and problems. Either you will walk in the blessings and enjoy all God has for you, or you will keep bringing forth trouble.

> ## Renewal Truth
>
> Search me, O God, and
> know my heart: try me, and
> know my thoughts.
> (Psalm 139:23 KJV)

If you set your mind on things above and are renewed in knowledge after the image of Jesus, you will stay on course with God's destiny for you.

STRUGGLE, STRUGGLE, STRUGGLE!

• Why do many Christians go through divorce? Go bankrupt? Stay sick? Get angry? Lie? We are supposed to be delivered from all of these problems, so why are they still going on? The answer is though we are saved, we haven't set our minds on things above and we haven't got our hearts right.

Why do many Christians struggle with their weight? Is it your hormones and your metabolism? Why do you fight in your marriage? Why can't some get their children to obey, or catch up on their financial obligations and get out of debt? The good man out of the good treasure of the heart brings forth good things, but the poor man out of the poor treasure of his heart keeps bringing forth poverty. What are we to do? We must get the heart right.

Some people say, "I love God. I am sincere. I'm telling you the truth, Pastor, my heart is right." In that sense the heart is right, but what thoughts are going on in the heart? It's not about being sincere or being a good person. It's about knowing what's going on with your thoughts.

•There are people who can't receive this teaching because they don't have a clue about what is going on inside their heads. If you don't have some awareness of what is happening in you, you can't even begin to understand this teaching. It takes honesty and openness to understand and then apply this teaching in your life.

When I first got saved, my mentor, Julius Young, said to me: "Casey, you don't even know what is going on in your own head." I wanted to act like I knew everything about the world, yet I was only nineteen. He said, "You not only don't know the world, you don't know yourself."

I said, "What are you talking about?"

He responded, "You are so unaware. You've got wrong thoughts and wrong attitudes."

Do you ever catch yourself being angry about something and you say, "Why did I get mad? What set me off today?" That's where you are unaware. Do you ever catch yourself in the refrigerator, choking down about 9,000 calories, and you are thinking, "My God, why am I doing this?" Or rationalizing one more day of cigarettes, thinking, "Why do I keep going through this?" Do you catch yourself skipping one more appointment at the exercise machine, and you wonder, "Why do I keep neglecting my exercise time?"

You see, you're so unaware of how you are thinking that you are doing things out of habit and out of those attitudes that are going on in your head, and you are not getting the fruit that you want. You keep doing it because you haven't plugged in to how to renew your mind, how to change your heart, or how to take hold of that tree so it starts producing the kind of fruit you want.

Renewal Truth

I am swift to hear, slow
to speak, and slow to wrath.
(James 1:19)

LOVING GOD WITH A "RIGHT" MIND

Just remember, out of the heart proceeds thoughts that will either bring blessing or cursing; that will either take you to the will of God or away from the will of God. If we love God with all our heart, it includes having our mind *stayed on Him.*

When the Pharisees asked Jesus, **Which is the great commandment in the law?** Jesus responded, **You shall love the Lord your God with all your heart, with all your soul, and with all your mind** (Matthew 22:36–37). Why did He say that? Because He wanted us to know that loving God doesn't mean just saying, "I love You, Lord," then going off and doing your own thing. It means getting our mind right.

"With all your heart" means with all your soul, and with all your mind. This means to *set your mind on things above.* It doesn't mean to think about heaven all day. It means to order your mind based on what God says in His Word.

Renewal Truth

I am hiding Your Word in
my heart, Lord, so I won't
sin against you.
(Psalm 119:11)

Jesus said, **Love the Lord your God with all your heart, with all your soul, and with all your mind** (Matthew 22:37). I have heard some people say, and I'm sure you have, too, "He really loves the Lord, but he just has this sin problem." "He really loves the Lord, but he can't whip the alcohol." "He really loves the Lord, but he just can't separate himself from adultery (or fornication)." "He loves God and he's a wonderful person, but he has an anger problem."

That's not true. If you love God with all your heart, that means with your soul, and it means your mind is right with God. If your mind is right with God, you won't have an anger problem, a drinking problem, or an adultery problem. You won't allow sin to rule your life because your mind is *stayed on Him*.

Renewal Truth

God keeps me in perfect peace, because my mind is focused on Him.
(Isaiah 26:3)

"I love God, but I'm afraid." You can't love God and be afraid at the same time, because perfect love casts out fear (1 John 4:18). If you love God with all your heart, soul and mind, your mind is stayed [focused] on Him and you will have perfect peace.

Setting your mind on the right things affects every aspect of life. When you begin to realize what your soul is doing to every aspect of your life, you will stop excusing and rationalizing: "God's will be done. He will do it in His time, and in His time He makes all things beautiful." No, it's when *you* get your mind stayed on Him.

Now, I'm not talking about mind games, mind over matter, and mental exercises. What I am saying is that biblically, *when your mind is right, your heart will be right.* When you love God with all your heart, things will be right. It's a good tree that produces good fruit. The good tree (person) starts working! The bills get paid, the kids obey, the marriage is fun, and everything happens for good.

Renewal Truth

God has not given me a spirit of fear, but He has given me power, love, and a sound mind.

(2 Timothy 1:7)

"But I'm just waiting on the Lord." No, He's waiting on you! He's waiting on you to love Him with all your heart, soul, and mind. Get your mind stayed on Him, and perfect peace will flow in your life.

SANCTIFIED BY THE WORD

3 John 2 says, *Beloved, I pray that you may prosper in all things and be in health, just as your soul prospers.* The King James Version says, *Beloved, I wish above all things that thou mayest prosper and be in health, even as thy soul prospereth.*

I believe this verse shows us several things. First, John wouldn't pray for you to prosper and be in health and record it in holy Scripture if it wasn't God's will. Second, the key to your prosperity "in all things" and being in health is *the well-being of your soul.*

How does the soul prosper? Verse 3 holds the answer: *For I rejoiced greatly when brethren came and testified of the truth that is in you, just as you walk in the truth.* The truth is the Word of God.

In John 17:17, Jesus said, *Sanctify them by Your truth. Your word is truth.* The Word is a sharp, two-edged sword that affects the heart, spirit, and soul. Truth causes your heart to prosper. It causes your soul to prosper. When your soul prospers, you will prosper in all things and live in health.

Keep your mind on Jesus, and you will have perfect peace. Love God with all your heart, soul, and mind, and all that God has for you will open up to you. Out of your heart you will start bringing forth prosperity because your soul is prospering. As the truth—God's Word—takes hold of your spirit and soul, your mind is renewed, your heart is renewed, and you will begin to prosper in all things, including your health.

In John 8:31–32, Jesus said, *If you abide in My word, you are My disciples indeed. And you shall know the truth, and the truth shall make you free.*

As you set your mind on the things of the Word, you will know the truth. Many Christians know more about their doctor and what he says than they do about what God says. They know more about what the lawyer says than what God says. They know more about what the talk show host says than they do about what God says. They know more about what the world says than they do about what the Word says. There isn't a lot of truth in their soul, so their soul isn't very prosperous. They can't prosper and be in health because their soul isn't prospering.

However, as you get into the Word and you know the truth, it will make you free. You will then prosper and be in health, even as your soul prospers.

Personal Application of
Renewal Truths

1. To keep from being controlled by wrong thoughts, I will:

   _____

   _____

   _____

   _____

2. I attract God's "best" blessings to me by believing: _____

   _____

   _____

   _____

   _____

3. I focus my mind on God by:_____

   _____

   _____

   _____

   _____

4. The prosperity of my spirit and body is proportionate to the prosperity of my _____ (3 John 2).

5. My soul prospers by (see 3 John 2): _____

   _____

   _____

6. I am sanctified by: _____

   _____

7. The truth of God's Word has set me free from: _____

    _____

    _____

    _____

    _____

8. I need the truth of God's Word to set me free from: _____

    _____

    _____

    _____

    _____

    _____

3

The Original State of Man: Undefiled and In God's Image

L et's go back to the book of Genesis and see how God taught Adam and Eve about the importance of aligning their thoughts with His words. At this point, *defilement* wasn't even in their vocabulary. They were perfect in the image of God.

Adam and Eve represented all of us back in the Garden of Eden. Theologically, we refer to Adam as the federal head of mankind. In other words, what he did has affected all of our lives.

Let's begin in Genesis, chapter 3:

Now the serpent was more cunning than any beast of the field which the Lord God had made. And he said to the woman, "Has God indeed said, 'You shall not eat of every tree of the garden'?" And the woman said to the serpent, "We may eat of the fruit of the trees of the garden; but of the fruit of the tree which is in the midst of the garden, God has said, 'You shall not eat it, nor shall you touch it, lest you die.'" Then the serpent said to the woman, "You will not surely die. For God knows that in the day you eat of it your eyes will be opened, and you will be like God, knowing good and evil."

So when the woman saw that the tree was good for food, that it was pleasant to the eyes, and a tree desirable to make one wise, she took of its fruit and ate. She also gave to her husband with her, and he ate.

Genesis 3:1–6

Adam was standing there the whole time. I used to believe that Adam was busy naming animals, but he was right there the entire time. He allowed the serpent to go on and on, then he ate with Eve.

Renewal Truth

I'll not be ensnared by
the lust of the flesh, the
lust of the eyes, or the
pride of life. Instead, I'll
be captivated and motivated
by God's Word.
(1 John 2:16)

Verse 7 says, **Then the eyes of both of them were opened.** Had they been walking around blind? What does "their eyes were opened" mean? It means they had new thoughts they had never had before. They had knowledge they didn't have previously.

The serpent wasn't more powerful, more beautiful, and more authoritative. Scripture says he was **more** *cunning.* We must realize that the power and authority of the devil and his demonic spirits isn't the problem we face today. But it's their cunning maneuvers, lies, trickery, and deceit that get us.

The serpent was cunning and he began to play with Eve's head: **You will not surely die. For God knows that in the day you eat of it** *your eyes will be opened, and you will be like God, knowing good and evil* (Genesis 3:4–5).

Adam and Eve were already like God. They were created in His image and likeness (Genesis 1:26). Eve was deceived with thoughts, because she didn't guard or discipline her mind. She didn't go to her husband and say, "Adam, what do you think? It sounds interesting." Adam didn't say, "Wait a minute. That's not true. We are already like God. Let's go talk to God and see what He has to say about this."

Adam and Eve let their minds get caught up in deception: "Yeah, we would be like God. He probably has been keeping something from us. Maybe there is more to life than God has told us."

They let the serpent's lie take rest in their minds. Remember, the lie of the devil is the opposite of the truth of the Word. If the Word brings you truth and the truth makes you free, a lie brings you into bondage and deception and keeps you bound. If a prosperous soul is full of the truth, then a poor soul is full of lies.

Renewal Truth

I am prospering in my spirit, soul, and body, and in my relationships and finances, because I am filled with God's truth.
(Joshua 1:8; Psalm 1:1–3)

EXPOSING SATAN'S LIES

Here's the bottom line for everyone who is struggling: *You are believing things the devil said, not what God said.* Here are three examples of the devil's lies:

The lie that will keep you in financial bondage: "Not everybody has to tithe, because tithing is a law." Tithing is a command (Malachi 3:8–12). You can believe a lie, but I'll believe the Word. Then let's see where you and I are, financially in ten years. The lie will bring bondage, but the truth will bring freedom.

The lie that can keep you sick: "God doesn't heal everybody." You can believe that if you want to, but I'm going to believe the Word. God is no respecter of persons (Acts 10:34). By Jesus' stripes you were already healed (1 Peter 2:24).

The lie that can ruin your family: "If my husband doesn't change, I will leave him. God wants me to be happy. If I have to divorce him to be happy, that's what I will do." Yet Scripture (truth) says God hates divorce (Malachi 2:16). It says to love your spouse and submit to one another (Ephesians 5:21–33).

The bottom line is: You can be caught up in a lie and as a result be entangled in all kinds of bondage. Or, you can be in agreement with the truth of God's Word and walk in absolute freedom.

In Eve's case, the serpent came along and said, "That's not what God meant." Eve bought it. So she and Adam ate and their eyes were opened. They began to think things they had never thought before and to know things they had not known previously, and the source of their knowledge was not God.

Renewal Truth

Believing Satan's lies and buying
into his deceptions bring bondage.
But believing the truth of
God's Word brings me into
absolute freedom.
(Galatians 5:1,13;
Psalm 119:45)

GRABBING FOR THE LEAVES!

Genesis 3:7 says that after their eyes were opened, *they knew that they were naked; and they sewed fig leaves together and made themselves coverings.* Isn't it interesting that as soon as they thought something that didn't come from God, they wanted to cover themselves and hide?

When you think things that don't come from God, you won't want Mom and Dad to know. Many children at an early age start hiding. Mom or Dad asks, "What are you doing?"

They respond, "Nothing."

Husbands and wives often do the same thing. They begin to hide and not talk about things. What are you covering? What is it you don't want to share? In a relationship where day after day things are covered up, division will eventually come. When things aren't from God, we cover.

Adam and Eve must have thought, "What are we doing naked in the garden?" Who cares? No one else was there. The weather was perfect. The chimpanzees weren't going to give them any trouble. They were the only humans there. But the sin nature is to "cover" when something isn't right.

Then, God shows up:

> *And they heard the sound of the Lord God walking in the garden in the cool of the day, and Adam and his wife hid themselves from the presence of the Lord God among the trees of the garden. Then the Lord God called to Adam and said to him, "Where are you?"*
>
> Genesis 3:8–9

When God asks a question, it's not because He doesn't already know the answer. It's because He wants you to think about the answer. He says, "Adam, what are you doing?"

Adam responds, "Nothing."

Adam and Eve's sin opened their minds to thoughts that didn't come from God. Up to this time, their thoughts were undefiled by anything of the world.

Renewal Truth

I choose to be undefiled
by sin, not because everything
that is hidden will be revealed,
but because I want to be like
Jesus.
(Matthew 10:26; 1 John 3:2)

THE "SOURCE" OF YOUR KNOWLEDGE

Adam said, *I heard Your voice . . . I was afraid because I was naked; and I hid myself. And He* [God] *said, "Who told you that you were naked?"* (Genesis 3:10–11). In other words, "Where did you even come up with that thought?"

Let's go back to chapter 2, verses 16 and 17, where the "off limits" tree was identified: *And the Lord God commanded the man, saying, "Of every tree of the garden you may freely eat; but of the tree of the knowledge of good and evil you shall not eat, for in the day that you eat of it you shall surely die."*

Isn't it interesting that this tree is about *knowledge*? It is about the thoughts of good and evil. Notice, God said it's a tree of the knowledge of *good* as well as evil. In every temptation there are things that are good. The issue isn't that it's good or even that it's evil, because God gave them the knowledge of good and evil. The issue is, *where are you getting your knowledge?* That's what the tree represents: the *source* of your thoughts.

God was saying, "I want the *source* of everything you think, everything you believe, and everything in your life to be Me. As long as it's Me, you've got it made in the shade. But the minute you turn to some other source—yourself, the devil, or the world—you are going to have problems and you will lose your relationship with Me. You're going to die spiritually, and then all kinds of curses will come upon you." And that's exactly what happened with Adam and Eve.

The key is not what you know, it's *how* you know it:

- Who told you that you can't get out of debt?
- Who told you that you're not smart?
- Who told you that you can't get a better job?
- Who told you that you can't make more money?
- Who told you that your company can't be bigger than it is?
- Who told you that your husband (or wife) won't change?
- Who told you that you're fat?
- Who told you that you're ugly?
- Who told you that you can't have a good marriage?
- Who told you that you've sinned too much to be forgiven?
- Who told you that you would never own your own home?
- Who told you that you can't be healed?

Begin to question the source of *every* thought. That was God's question of Adam: **Who told you that you were naked?** (Genesis 3:11).

Don't you think God would have told Adam and Eve about good and evil and talked to them about anything they wanted to know? If Adam had asked, "God, what does *naked* mean?" don't you think God would have told him? The problem was, Adam went to the devil instead of to the Lord.

We want our children to know the difference between good and evil. We will tell them what's going on, the bad side as well as the good side, but we don't want them to go to the bad side to find out firsthand what is bad. The *source* of their knowledge is the key to their destiny. If they know about good and evil from godly instruction, they will prosper in their soul. But if they know about good and evil because they've been in the gutter finding out from the world, they will have hurts, pains, and turmoil that will drag them down for years to come.

Renewal Truth

God is the source of my
knowledge. In Him I live and
move and have my being.
Obedience to His direction
is the key to the fulfillment
of my divine destiny.
(Acts 17:28; 1 Samuel 15:22)

I want my sons and my daughter to know about sex. I talk to them about sex, and they don't even want to talk about it yet, but there is going to come a day when they will be interested. I'm talking to them about it now because I want them to get the knowledge of sex from a godly perspective. I don't want them to get the knowledge of sex from the back seat of a car, from a *Playboy* magazine, or from some other secular humanist health teacher.

Knowledge from worldly sources will hurt them. The knowledge I give them about sex will be from God's perspective—from God's Word—and that knowledge will bless them.

In the past, the Church tried to keep people in the dark about sex. We talk about everything but sex from God's perspective. The tree of the knowledge of life is truth and it brings freedom. But the knowledge of good and evil is deceptive, cunning, twisted, and perverted. While there's some good in it, the evil in it will bring bondage.

Most people who are struggling in their sexual relationship are struggling because much of what they think about sex came from the tree of the knowledge of good and evil. It didn't come from the tree of life from God. It came from the world. It doesn't make you evil, but it just means you have some thoughts that are binding you up, holding you back, and keeping you from God's perfect will.

If you're struggling with sex, with finances, with relationships, or with children, you have knowledge that came from the tree of the knowledge of good and evil. You are operating off of thoughts that came from this world rather than from God, and those thoughts will keep you in bondage until you renew your mind with God's Word.

The question is, who told you that you can't communicate? Who told you that you're not good at sharing your feelings? When you start doubting every lie of the devil, you will start getting free.

When you start questioning everything the world tells you, you will start getting free: "Wait a minute, that thought came from the devil. That thought came from the tree of the knowledge of good and evil. I don't buy that. I'm only accepting the thoughts that come from God." Then your soul will start to prosper. Your mind will start to be renewed. You are setting your mind on things above, not on the things of the world, and all of a sudden, the blessings of God start coming upon you.

Renewal Truth

I am standing fast in the
liberty Christ has provided
for me. I'll not be entangled
again with the bondage of
believing Satan's lies.
(Galatians 5:1)

Who told you that you have a temper? Where did you get that thought? Don't believe it. You simply have bad thinking. Your temper isn't any different than anyone else's temper. But, you've got an attitude because of thoughts that somebody from the tree of the knowledge of good and evil put in your mind.

Look at any area of your life where you believe you have a problem and ask yourself, "Where did I get that thought? What thoughts have I been operating from? What thoughts have been controlling me?"

We like to blame Satan for taking our jobs, our spouses, and our health, and certainly he is the source of *all evil*. But don't just blame the *source*. Look at *how you let it come into your life*.

When a mouse is in my house, I know a mother mouse birthed that little critter, but the mother mouse is not my problem. The problem is, *how did he get in my house?* There is a devil and you know he is the ultimate source of every problem, but that's not the real issue. The issue is, *how did the problem get into your life?* If you plug the hole, you don't care how many mother mice are out there! As long as they aren't in your house, the mother mice can do whatever they want to do. When you plug the hole in your life, the

44

devil can do whatever he wants to do, but he won't be able to get in! None of his antics will affect you!

Renewal Truth

Because I am submitted to
God, I resist the enemy and
he flees from me.
(James 4:7)

DISCIPLINING THE MIND WITH GOD'S WORD

Paul said, *For though we walk in the flesh, we do not war according to the flesh* (2 Corinthians 10:3). We live in a fleshly body and a carnal, physical world, but we don't war according to the flesh. In other words, don't make things in the physical world around you the issues that you are struggling with.

In our church we don't preach about hair and clothes and all that stuff, because that's not where the battle is. If you want to color your hair, or paint your face, just do what you are going to do. Be modest and reasonable, but recognize that's not the issue. When you get into the fleshly battles and everything becomes a physical issue, you are off track.

When little kids are worried about their physical body, we say to them, "Come on, you're going to grow up. Don't worry. Don't even think about it. Everything is going to be cool! Get your mind educated. Learn to serve God and that won't be a problem."

As adults we need to learn this lesson, because we spend an hour primping our body and two seconds plugging into the Spirit. We have time to shower, shave, paint, color, comb, brush, spray and rub, but we have little or no time to pray. Don't let your fleshly, physical being take center stage in your life.

> *For the weapons of our warfare are not carnal* [physical, fleshly] *but mighty in God for pulling down strongholds.*
>
> 2 Corinthians 10:4

If I stopped right here and started talking about the strong-holds of the devil, you would shout, for most Christians are into this: "Yeah, we need to pull down the strongholds of the devil. We need to speak to the prince of the power of the air and go after the demons in the spirit realm. We need to do warfare and wrestle against principalities and powers." We get all fired up about this stuff, because it's an ethereal [or intangible] thing that doesn't make us look at our practical lives.

Are you a better wife? "No, but I broke the power of the devil." Did you pay any bills? "No, but I went into the third heaven." Did you clean your house? "Yeah, I got the spirits out of there." Why don't you just deal with the garbage? We like to talk about the strongholds and spiritual things, but what are they?

Second Corinthians 10:5 says:

> *Casting down arguments* [*The King James Version* says imagina-tions] *and every high thing that exalts itself against the knowl-edge of God, bringing every thought into captivity to the obedi-ence of Christ.*

Paul is not talking about demons. He is talking about argu-ments, imaginations, reasonings, thoughts, and knowledge. These are the strongholds that keep us from winning the war and from being the people God wants us to be. We are dealing with the same thing that we dealt with back in the Garden of Eden. Satan wasn't the problem. Adam opened their minds to the thoughts, deceptions, and lies of the devil. They could have kicked the devil out of the garden with their little pinkies. They could have stepped on the serpent and stomped his head! They could have roasted him and had their first meal of meat.

Adam and Eve had the authority and dominion of God over every beast of the field. They could have wrung the serpent's neck and had a gourmet dinner, but their heads got in the way. The strongholds that caused them to sin were deception, fleshly ideas, and lies. These strongholds removed them from the blessing of God and got them kicked out of the Garden of Eden.

Although Satan is the father of all lies (John 8:44), ultimately he and his demons are not your problem because he is already defeated through Jesus' cross. The way you win the war over his strongholds is by getting your mind renewed to the Word of God and not buying into his lies and deceptions, not allowing arguments and worldly knowledge to be exalted against the knowledge of God.

When you get your mind disciplined with the Word, you will win every war! That is where you will find freedom, abundant life, and the blessings of God. By being transformed by the renewing of your mind with God's Word, you will find God's perfect will.

Renewal Truth

God *always* causes me to
triumph in Christ.
(2 Corinthians 2:14)

When revival hits, if your mind is still all messed up, it won't have a great impact upon your life. Many of us have gone to conferences, services, and meetings where we got in the glory cloud. Glory balls and hot oil were busted over our heads, and we fell out under the power of God. We laughed until our stomachs hurt. Then we went home and the wife still hates the husband, the kids are still rebelling, the bills still aren't paid, and we are still thirty-five pounds overweight. We look in the mirror and we are still ugly. We think, "We've got to go back to the glory balls, back to the cloud, back to the anointing, and have the evangelist pray for us again."

Thank God for the miracles and for His presence, but if we aren't renewing our minds with God's Word, nothing is going to change. If we aren't renewing our minds with God's Word, we will never win the war.

I can cast the devil out of someone who needs deliverance, but I cannot cast out their thoughts, reasonings, and imaginations. Demons will obey me, but my head won't. That's why you can pray against these things and rebuke them, but there will be no lasting change until you renew your mind to God's Word.

Case in point: smoking. Most people start smoking because they are trying to look cool. Then they find out that cigarettes are killing them, so they want to quit. So, how are they going to quit? Rebuke a nicotine demon. Right? We've all heard this. Brother So-and-so prays and casts out a nicotine demon. But the next morning your cup of coffee isn't right without a cigarette. Or, you can't go back to work after lunch without a cigarette. Or, you go all day without a cigarette, then after dinner when you have your latte, you think, "After all day I deserve a cigarette. Brother So-and-so cast a demon out of me and he's a man of God, a man of authority. How come I'm thinking about cigarettes again?"

Some people blame their genetic makeup: "I'm just one of those people who have more addictive behavioral problems because of my genetic makeup." We love this! We've got fat genes, addictive genes, alcohol genes, heroin genes, thief genes, and because of our "genetic makeup" we are not responsible. Christians blame the devil. Secular humanists don't believe in a devil, because that would be too spooky, so they blame your genes. And if it's not your genes, it's your corduroys, or your Levis!!

What has to happen to whip this thing? There are genetic issues, but I'm convinced God gave us the power to rule over our flesh. The war is not with our genetic makeup. A renewed mind will change your physical body. When you get your mind renewed, then you're not going to suck on cigarettes anymore. You can replace cigarettes, but it all comes back to one issue: *When my thinking changes, then I'll break the habit.*

At nineteen I was in a drug rehabilitation center. I had quit smoking pot, snorting coke, and sticking needles in my arm. And it's all because one day I asked myself, "Why am I doing this?" My thinking about cigarettes and drugs changed. I no longer needed them to feel good or to look good. I was really tired of yellow fingernails and green teeth! It's a bummer, because kissing a smoker is like kissing an ash tray! I was trying to find someone to kiss me, you know, so I needed to clean up.

When my thinking about cigarettes changed, I quit smoking in one day. No patches. No pills. No packs of gum.

So what's the key to pulling down strongholds and breaking old habits? *Capturing every thought and bringing it into obedience to Christ.* If you will train yourself to capture thoughts and bring them into agreement with God's Word, you can kick cigarettes or any other habit.

The stronghold is in your thoughts, and when those thoughts from the world—from the tree of the knowledge of good and evil—have a stronghold on you, that's the area that has to be renewed.

Personal Application of
Renewal Truths

1. I accept God's Word as the highest standard of truth in the following areas of my life: _____

   _____

   _____

   _____

2. To be created in God's image and likeness means: _____

   _____

   _____

   _____

   _____

3. The power and authority of Satan and his demonic spirits isn't the challenge we face today. It is their _____

   _____

   _____

4. Lies bring _____, but truth brings

   _____.

5. The source of my thoughts, words, and actions is: _____

   _____

6. I am closing the door so the devil will have *no entrance* into my life to influence me or contaminate my thoughts by:

   _____

   _____

   _____

   _____

   _____

   _____

7. Our battles are won or lost in the arena of the _____.

8. I am bringing my thoughts into obedience to Christ by:

   _____

   _____

   _____

   _____

   _____

   _____

4

Replacing Negative Habits

W hile driving to church one evening, my son Caleb said, "Dad, they ought to let ten-year-olds drive."

I said, "Boy, that would be a wild thing."

He said, "Well then at least twelve-year-olds. I can drive better than a lot of people I know." He's probably right!

Caleb is learning and growing, and inside of him is a desire to get bigger and better and to do more. As adults, our desires may be buried under fears and failures, but there is still a desire to be like your Father. The Bible says we were predestined to be conformed to the image of Jesus Christ. There is a desire in all of us for continual growth and transformation. I want to change. I want to be like Jesus who submitted to the will of the Father, and even when they hung Him on a tree, He obeyed God.

The spirit of the natural man wants to argue and fight. I have counseled couples who were ready to divorce because of fighting and screaming over the color of towels in the bathroom. We've all heard the jokes of people arguing over which way the toilet paper is supposed to hang, rolled out or rolled in. Simple solution: Just get two rolls and do one each way!

Many people come to our church and I know we tell them the truth, but some don't come back because they don't want to hear it. They don't want to change their habits.

A habit is a thought or a way of thinking that causes us to function in the same routines all of our adult life. It is a repeated thought or behavior that becomes so automatic that it is difficult to stop. It can become an addiction, a custom, or a tradition.

Most of our habits, whether good or bad, were picked up by watching the habits of those around us. If kids grow up where Mom and Dad take showers, comb their hair, and dress properly, most likely they will do the same thing.

The Bible says in Proverbs 22:6, *Train up a child in the way he should go, and when he is old he will not depart from it.* When he is young, he may depart from it for a while, but he will come back to the teachings of his early childhood.

TIME-RELEASED BELIEFS

Have you done things for a season in your life that were contrary to the habits of your parents, but then somewhere around thirty or thirty-five, you realized how much like your parents you had become? When children grow up, they won't depart from what they were taught. I call their habits "time-released beliefs."

Usually, when you start to do something that becomes a habit, it's not easy at first, but you do it repeatedly until it becomes easy. The first cigarette doesn't taste good, although you try to act cool. You turn green, cough, and vomit. But many people keep at it until it becomes a habit. Other people get in the habit of watching soap operas.

For more than twenty years I've gone to a little restaurant in the Seattle area that makes good ribs. You can only go there about once every six months, because it takes that long to get the fat and cholesterol out of your system! You can tell they are good ribs because the floor is so greasy you just slide in there! So I slide in and get a pound of pork ribs—the small ends that fall off the bone—and some white bread.

Every time I go there they've got a TV on and they're watching "As My Stomach Turns," or some soap opera. Those guys love me. They say, "Praise the Lord, Pastor. It's been a long time since you've been here. How's the church doing? Has the Lord been good to you? Good to see you. You're going to have the usual? Small end? Praise the Lord!"

Now, how can you be praising God, working in your business, and watching "All My Hopelessness," "The Terrible Hospital," and "As My Stomach Turns"? They know the characters on the shows as well as they know me. It's a habit. It's a stronghold.

Christians can have negative, worldly habits just like non-Christians. It's a way of thinking and acting that you repeat until it becomes a part of your life.

You can develop habits with sex, money, and food. Habits are formed by repeated thoughts and actions. They have nothing to do with good or bad, right or wrong. If you think something and do it repeatedly, it will become a habit.

Your spirit, soul, and body are designed to grasp things and hang on to them. God's idea is that we get the Word of God in us, hang on to it, and not let it go. But if we pump the world into us, the same thing will happen.

God's plan was that He would fill Adam so full of the truth that he would hang onto it and live that truth forever. That was His plan for all mankind.

THE "PROCESS" OF BREAKING HABITS

One great thing about being a born-again person is that you can break old habits. You can stop the process. You can turn the repeated thoughts and behavior around.

How long does it take to turn negative habits around? I believe a minimum of forty days. God gave us a mark at forty. Moses was forty days on the mountain. Jesus was forty days in the wilderness. I believe it will take you forty days to get anything going, but even then, you can backslide in a hurry. Generally, it takes two or three years to make something a part of your life. Forty days will get you started. Then, after two or three years, it will become a part of your life.

Most people just want a touch to break a habit. You can get that too, but that's just step one. After you fall to the floor from the power of God, you've got to get up. Getting you on the floor is not hard, but it's what happens when you get up that we're worried about.

Many people who receive a touch from heaven go back to their bad habits. A day later they have a cigarette. Two days later they have another beer. Three days later they're yelling at their wife, yet they fell out under the power of God and said, "Thank God, I'm delivered from anger." A week later they are yelling at their kids, kicking the cat, and slamming the door.

We spend years doing certain things, then we want them changed overnight. We follow the devil twenty-seven years, come to God, and say, "Straighten me out, Lord." We spend years with bad eating habits and we want everything to be different in thirty days or less, and that's just not realistic. A long-term follow-through is needed.

Most of our habits are picked up by watching the habits of those around us. We hear an accent and pretty soon we are talking like the people we are around. When I go overseas, I talk differently, according to the country I am in. This is the reason we've got to be so careful about who we hang out with. Soon we'll smell like them, sound like them, and be like them.

Renewal Truth

I am a companion of those
who keep God's Word.
(Psalm 119:63)

If you are having a problem with finances, check who you are hanging out with. If you are having a problem with your health, check who you are hanging out with. If you have a problem with your temper, who are you hanging out with?

REPLACING NEGATIVE HABITS WITH POSITIVE ONES

Habits are not so much stopped as they are *replaced*. It's not just a matter of stopping the negative, it's a matter of developing something positive to replace the negative.

Foolish parents say to their children, "Don't do that." Wise parents say, "Come over here and do this." When you say, "Don't do that," a child's immediate response is, "Why?" Wise parents *replace* the thought and the action.

When a child is near breakable objects, instead of saying, "Don't touch that," say, "Look at this stuffed animal. Let's play with it." Replace what you don't want them to have with something they can have.

If I preach all day on what you shouldn't do, all you will do when you go out of church is think about everything you shouldn't do. This is why we preach on righteousness rather than on sin.

Renewal Truth

I am the righteousness
of God in Christ Jesus.
(2 Corinthians 5:21)

Smoking isn't a big deal, but it's better to replace it with positive health habits like breathing! Eating Cheetos isn't a big deal, but it's better to replace them with fruit and vegetables and "real" food. Rather than stopping the negative, we want to replace it. You can replace overeating with, "I'm going to get healthy"; anger with, "I'm going to start being kind"; and cursing with, "I'm going to speak words of grace." If you focus on what you are stopping, you will probably never stop it.

A wise coach doesn't say to his player, "Stop swinging the bat that way." Instead he says, "Swing the bat at this level." Get the person focused on what you want, not on what you don't want.

Philippians 4:8 says:

> *Finally, brethren, whatever things are true, whatever things are noble, whatever things are just, whatever things are pure, whatever things are lovely, whatever things are of good report, if there is any virtue and if there is anything praiseworthy—meditate on these things.*

Notice, it doesn't state all the things that you are *not* supposed to think about. It lists the things you are to focus on. Breaking a habit is not stopping something as much as it is starting something.

KEYS TO BREAKING OLD HABITS AND BUILDING NEW ONES

Some of the keys to breaking old habits and building new ones are:

Key #1: *Desire something different.*

Desire sparks change. I desire windows that are not yellow from smoke, and fingers and teeth that are not green. I desire lungs that are not black. When you desire something you didn't desire before, you are ready to break an old habit and start a new one. If there is no desire, nothing is going to happen.

Psalm 37:4 says:

Delight yourself also in the Lord, and He shall give you the desires of your heart.

When you desire to be healthy, you will begin to change your eating and exercise habits. As long as there is no desire for a long life of health and fitness, you can buy the books, tapes, equipment, programs, and vitamins, but there will be no change. The beginning of your change is the *desire* to change.

Key #2: *Begin to picture yourself with that new thought, action, and lifestyle.*

The hardest thing for me to do when I became a Christian was to see myself never using drugs, never drinking alcohol, and never having to go to a chemical substance for some kind of feeling. I was a Christian and hadn't used drugs for almost a year before I could really see myself making that change.

Now the difference between me and most of the people around me at that time was that they weren't working on a new picture, so they lived drug-free for a year and then went right back to it. What about the person who loses fifty pounds and then gains sixty? They never get a new picture. They may change for a season, but they never get a new picture of themselves in their mind.

For almost a year I worked on a new perspective of myself: "I will build new and better relationships. I will find satisfaction from new and different sources. I am free from my past." This means that I will never smoke another cigarette; I will never smoke another joint; I will never snort another line of coke; I'll never stick another needle in my arm.

Most people never get to the place where they get a "new picture" of themselves. Though they may change for a season, without a new picture, they go right back to their old habits.

Renewal Truth

I am framing my life with what God says about me in His Word. He says He has a future and a hope for me, filled with peace and free of evil.
(Hebrews 11:3; Jeremiah 29:11)

It's like the guy with a temper. He says, "I'm not going to shout, yell, or scream. I'm going to stay cool." He has a heart attack and dies because he didn't get a new picture of himself. He held his feelings inside. What he should have done was to say, "I'm a kind, gentle person. I see myself communicating, not yelling. I see myself listening and understanding, not angrily controlling. I see myself building intimacy in relationships, not pushing others away."

This new picture of himself could have enabled him to walk free of anger rather than to keep it bottled up inside.

For lifestyle issues, we are talking about months of consistenty changing the way we think and months of looking at the "new you."

Out of nearly 3,000 young people who entered the drug rehab program, I was one of the few who completed it. Today I can count less than a dozen of those people who stayed clean. The others didn't change their picture of themselves.

Joshua 1:8 is the Scripture for Key #2:

This Book of the Law shall not depart from your mouth, but you shall meditate in it day and night, that you may observe to do according to all that is written in it. For then you will make your way prosperous, and then you will have good success.

Key #3: *Talk about the way you want to be, not the way you are.*

Start communicating in a new way. Instead of saying things like, "It makes me so mad," say, "I am beginning to understand another point of view." You have to speak new words before you will get new feelings. You have to say things like, "I used to live for my next meal, but now food isn't that important to me." Your desire is, "Give me something to eat," but your words are, "You know, food isn't that important to me anymore."

Jesus said:

For assuredly, I say to you, whoever says to this mountain, "Be removed and be cast into the sea," and does not doubt in his heart, but believes that those things he says will be done, he will have whatever he says.

Mark 11:23

What have you been saying? "I can't believe how hard it is. This diet is killing me." If that's not what you want, don't say it.

"I've been trying to quit smoking, but I'm telling you, every time I look around, somebody is lighting up, and it is driving me crazy." If that's not what you want, don't say it. What you need to say is, "It's easy to quit smoking." You may not feel that way. In fact, you're getting ready to smoke the carpet in your car! But you say, "To quit smoking is no big deal. I'll whip it easily." *Start speaking what you desire to achieve.*

Renewal Truth

Like the example God gave me, I will call those things which do not exist as though they did. They will manifest because God cannot lie. He will make good on *all* of His promises.
(Romans 4:17; Numbers 23:19)

You can say, "Losing weight is easy for me, because my metabolism is right. I am designed to lose weight and I can take it off!" In their struggle to lose weight, some people lay hands on the scale and say, "Be healed, in Jesus' name!" Others say, "I didn't eat anything for three months and I gained two pounds." Or, "Everything I eat goes right on my belly!" We're not talking about just stopping something. We are talking about replacing the negative with something new and different. If you make a decision to turn the power to remain negative, into a power to be positive, your entire life will change.

Key #4: *Practice thinking and doing the new thing every day.*

Repetition makes something a part of you. Anything you want to be good at, you have to practice. "Wishing" something was different won't bring the change. You have to practice. If you want to play golf and be good at it, you have to practice. If you want to play baseball and be good at it, you have to practice. Many people want the change, but they don't want the practice that goes with it.

Practice your new thoughts every day. Spend five or ten minutes a day seeing yourself as a new person. Say it out loud to yourself: "I am that new person. I am a kind, gentle, and patient person." Make your new thoughts, confessions, and actions a normal part of your daily behavior. If you only work on it on Sundays when you go to church, then not much is going to change. Six days of doing your old thing and one day of trying something new won't make much difference. James 1:25 says you will be blessed in what you do. The more you practice the "new you," the more change will come, the more blessings will come, and the more renewal will come.

Many times it's helpful to get two or three friends to interact with you as you practice so you can be a help and support to each other. If you hang around people who are doing what you are doing, they will be an encouragement to you.

Key #5: *You have to get to the place where the new thing is "normal" in your mind.*

If it never gets to the place where it is normal, then you won't change. It's normal for me to wake up early and pray, but it's abnormal for me to say, "Wow! I'm telling you, today I was in the Holy

Ghost!" That's not the real me. It's an aberration because it's not normal. Waking up early and seeking God in the morning is normal to me. Giving is normal to me. It's part of my lifestyle. I do it all the time, like breathing. Patience and kindness are normal to me. It's normal for me to be a leader and set the pace for others to follow. You have to get your routine into your mind until you say, "That's the way I am."

Renewal Truth

As I think in my heart,
so am I. I see myself victorious
in Christ Jesus in achieving
the destiny God has set before me.
(Proverbs 23:7; 1 Corinthians 15:57)

When you step up to the plate and hit a home run and say, "Did you see that?" then we know that's not normal for you. That was unusual for you. When you do something good and someone goes, "Wow! You've really changed," you respond, "That's just the way I am."

"I remember before, you'd have been throwing a fit right now, slamming the door, and kicking the cat."

"But this is the way I am. It's normal to me now." You have to make it part of you so that it's no longer something that you are hoping for.

Key #6: *When you backslide, get up and go on without condemnation.*

When you fail, fall, stumble, or go back on your old routine, stop and continue on from where you left off. Don't go all the way back to the beginning, because you've made a lot of progress. Just get up and go on, free of condemnation.

The devil will say, "You blew it. You haven't changed a thing. You're really the same old person. Look at you. You talk about being patient and kind. Now you've gone off and put your fist through the wall again." Patch it up, or hang a picture over the hole, and get back to your routine of, "I'm a kind, gentle, and patient person." One step back doesn't mean you've lost it all, so don't let the devil condemn you.

Renewal Truth

I will not receive condemnation,
because I no longer walk according
to the flesh. I am a child of God,
and I am led by His Spirit.
(Romans 8:1,14)

Many people mess up on their way to the "new you." They may be on a new eating program and they've lost five pounds. They feel good about themselves. Then one day they eat a bag of Cheetos and say, "I blew it!" You haven't lost everything. Pick up from where you left off and keep right on going, recognizing that a few missteps are a normal part of the process. That doesn't mean you should excuse it to the point you take a step back every day, but if it happens, don't let it be the end of your journey. Pick up and press on, saying, "That's really not like me. I'm not going to do that again. I am moving on."

If you carry guilt and condemnation, you are preparing to repeat that behavior again. But when you really decide to move on, let it go and go on about your business.

Key #7: *Be alert to past weaknesses that may pop up again.*

Usually what happens is, once you've had some success, you relax and the tendency is to slip back into the old behaviors again. Right after David had won a great victory for Israel, instead of going out with his troops as he should have done, he stayed home, and rose from bed in the middle of the day. Looking from the roof of his house he spied Bathsheba as she was bathing on a nearby rooftop.

As a result of his affair with Bathsheba and his plot to kill her husband, which was carried out, he entered into one of the greatest seasons of pain and defeat of his life, right after one of his greatest victories. (See 2 Samuel, chapter 11.)

As you make progress, don't allow yourself to slip back into some of your old habits or routines. This is where people get into the cycle of ups and downs. Habits are like ruts in a road. It's easy to slip into the ruts, but it's harder to get out of them. To stay out of them takes a conscious effort, but to get into them takes little or no effort.

When I was a kid, we used to ride motorcycles on a military reservation. Before it was a military reservation, there were many homes, orchards, and farms on the property. There were many old roads, driveways, and cartways that had been grown over with weeds, but we knew that we could still get through on our horses and motorcycles. We could reopen old roads much easier than we could build new ones.

In your attitudes and mind-sets, you will reopen old roads much easier than building new ones. So be alert to keep from slipping into some of the old routines again.

Remember, we talked briefly about "time-released beliefs," where attitudes surface that you had no idea were a part of you, because as a young person they weren't a part of your lifestyle.

But when you hit thirty-five, suddenly you start acting like your mom. When you hit forty, you start talking about things that you picked up from your parents. At fifty, you start saying things that you had never thought before. Suddenly, you realize that you are talking like people in your past. That's what I call "time-released beliefs."

We have a video where I am giving Caleb a bath the day he was born. A few minutes after his birth in our home, I had him in the sink. Later, I watched this video and realized I was talking just like my dad. I never talked like that before, but I'd never been a dad before. So at the moment of my son's birth, a time-released belief went off in me. I picked up thoughts and behaviors and words that I'd heard from my father and began to repeat them to my son. That caused me to realize I'd better plug in here, because I would probably discipline him the way I was disciplined without even thinking about it. I would probably do things with him the way things were done with me without even thinking about it. There are some great things that I got from my dad, but I needed to be alert to time-released beliefs.

If you are in your twenties or thirties, age is not a great concern to you yet. But when you are sixty, your attitude about age will surface and you'll start saying and doing things that you never thought were inside of you. That's why we need to be real serious about programming ourselves to say what God says about us.

Everyone around us is dying at seventy or eighty. They are not planning to live beyond that age. They're middle-aged at forty and are preparing to die at sixty. If they make it to seventy or eighty, they're talking about how they really had a good life. If you're going to go beyond that, you have generations of thoughts, words, and attitudes to break.

Fred Price from Crenshaw Christian Center in Los Angeles taught me years ago that God gave me 120 years. Genesis 6:3 says, "The years of man are 120." So I began to program myself, "I'm going for 120." I'm not going to be middle-aged at forty or fifty. At sixty, I will celebrate middle age. You have to program it into your mind and come against those time-released beliefs.

When some people hit forty, they say, "I'm over the hill now." No! I'm still on my way up. That's why at forty I'm doing more new things than I did when I was twenty, things I've never done before, stretching myself physically, mentally, and spiritually beyond where I've ever been before. I'm still on my way up! When I'm sixty I will say, "Now I'm at the top of the hill." Then I can start floating into the last half of my life. Of course, I won't float, but you understand what I'm saying. It's a whole new mind-set. You have to fight the old belief and most people don't have the guts to fight it. They just fall into it and do what they were raised to do.

We may not get the benefits of what we are committed to in the areas of change and renewal, but we can pass something on to the next generation so they can go beyond us. If we hand them the ability to get out of the rut, out of the routine, and not get stuck in the old ways, then we've done them a great service. We're not just living for ourselves, we're living for the next generations. We're not just doing this for what we get, but for what we can give.

Years ago T. L. Osborn said to me, "I may not make 120, but if I reach for it, maybe somebody following me will make it. If I don't reach for it, they probably won't reach for it either." Someone has to start the process and break the norm, then pass it on.

Personal Application of
Renewal Truths

1. Identify negative habits in your own life that you want to see replaced with positive habits:

   Negative Habit　　　　*Positive Replacement*

   _____　　_____
   _____　　_____
   _____　　_____
   _____　　_____
   _____　　_____
   _____　　_____
   _____　　_____

2. Instead of focusing on negative habits, I will focus on things that are (see Philippians 4:8):
   a. *True*
   b. *Honorable*
   c. *Pure*
   d. *Lovely*
   e. *Admirable*
   f. *Excellent*
   g. *Worthy of Praise*
   h. *Just*

3. I am speaking what I desire to achieve, which is: _____
   _____
   _____
   _____
   _____

4. Daily practicing new thoughts about myself will: _____

_____

_____

_____

_____

5

Truth Exposes the Devil's Strongholds

Be sober, be vigilant; because your adversary the devil walks about like a roaring lion, seeking whom he may devour.

1 Peter 5:8

Satan is the source of all evil, but his power is limited. He can't do anything he wants, nor can he touch just anybody he wants to touch. He is *seeking* whom he may devour. That tells us that he can only devour the lives of those who will allow him to do so.

We must be sober, self-controlled, vigilant, and watchful because Satan is constantly on the prowl, seeking someone to devour. 1 Peter 5:9, says: *Resist him, steadfast in the faith, knowing* . . . . In other words, what you know is a major part of resisting the devil. Resisting him in the faith means that you can resist him with the Word, because faith comes by hearing, and hearing by the Word of God (Romans 10:17). If you don't know the Word, you can't resist the devil, steadfast in the faith.

There is no resistance to the devil available in sermons from secular magazines or newspapers. We must have truth (God's Word) working in us to resist the devil and his lies.

A bank teller is trained to recognize counterfeit money, not by handling the counterfeit, but by handling the "real" stuff! We don't need to spend time studying cults to recognize them. If we know the Word, we will be able to recognize the devil's lies, in whatever form they come.

I'm not going to teach my children how to smoke pot so they will recognize it. I am going to teach them how to live righteously. As a result, they will understand anything that is unrighteous. *If you are full of the Word, you will understand anything that is not of the Word.*

Years ago I had a friend who taught comparative religions in churches and did seminars on the occult. He came to a point when he went totally bonkers. He was depressed and discouraged. I asked him, "Man, what is going on?" He said, "I have spent so much time talking about what is wrong, it has destroyed my faith. I am not going to do any more seminars. I am doing nothing but reading the Word, getting my relationship back with God, and plugging in to the truth." Truth will keep you free. If you talk about lies long enough, they will bring you into bondage.

Jesus said in John 10:10 that Satan comes to steal, kill, and destroy. But what has to happen before he can do that and get away with it? He has to get us to believe a lie. He has to steal truth from us. If Satan can get you to believe a lie about your spouse, he can destroy your marriage. One such lie is, "He [or she] is not going to change, and you deserve to be happy. Leave him [or her] and get on with your life."

You start thinking, "That's right." Then you have to spiritualize a lie: "Doesn't God want me to be happy? If God wants me to be happy, then He must want me to leave my husband [or wife] because the only way I can be happy is to get away from him [her]." Now a lie, made to sound Christlike, is running your life.

You always have to find a co-signer for a lie, so you find a friend and say, "I've been thinking about leaving my husband because the Lord wants me to be happy." The friend is sober and vigilant, so she says, "Sister, you are way off base. God called you to a lifetime commitment. God is going to bless your marriage. He is going to change your marriage. Scripture says you can sanctify your husband. Let's believe and pray the Word and turn this thing around."

You are looking for someone to co-sign your lie, and your friend keeps bringing you the truth, so you go to another friend. "I think God wants me to leave my husband. Doesn't God want me to be happy?" You've found someone who has the same lie working in them. She has an ugly husband, too. So this person says, "I think you are right. There is no condemnation in Christ, and God has not called us to bondage. I think you'd better leave that chump. You will probably be better off without him." Now you've got a co-signer. Two of you agree and you start acting on the lie.

The same thing happens when you decide you are not going to tithe or you are not going to be committed to a church. Most of the time people do not leave a church by themselves. They leave in groups because they don't have the guts to act on a lie by themselves. They have to find a co-signer to act on their lie. Sometimes people leave their church so they can get rid of their spouse. Or they leave their church so they can stop serving and giving. Be alert to people who are looking for a co-signer for their lie.

Renewal Truth

If the truth sets you free,
then lies will bring you into
bondage.
(John 8:31–32)

HOW JESUS HANDLED THE DEVIL'S LIES

In Matthew, chapter 4, Jesus gives us an example of how to handle the devil's lies and deceptions.

Then Jesus was led up by the Spirit into the wilderness to be tempted by the devil. And when He had fasted forty days and forty nights, afterward He was hungry. Now when the tempter came to Him, he said, "If You are the Son of God, command that these stones become bread."

Matthew 4:1–3

This lie questions Jesus' identity: *If You are the Son of God.* The voice of God had already revealed Jesus' identity: *This is My beloved Son, in whom I am well pleased* (Matthew 3:17). Satan's question was to the voice of God and to the Word of God.

What happens when you get thoughts, such as:

- "If I was healed, it seems like I'd feel better."
- "If God wanted to prosper my life, it seems like I'd have more money."
- "If the Word was true, it seems like things would be different."

Satan does the same thing to you that he did to Jesus. "If you are the Son of God, do something to prove it." He was planting a seed of doubt and unbelief by asking Jesus to prove His identity.

Remember, Genesis 3:1 said, *The serpent was more cunning than any beast of the field.* The issue here with Jesus' confrontation by the devil isn't about power; it's about his *ability to lie and deceive.*

Satan has been stripped of his authority, but he has some power. It is his subtleties that we have to deal with. You can wipe out his power with the name of Jesus the same day you are saved! That doesn't mean you are smart enough to keep from being tricked, deceived, or lied to, which is the issue. We are so worried about having power over the devil that we fail to realize, that is *not* the problem. We've got power over the devil, but if he lies to us and we are dull in our thinking and hearing, he is able to succeed in deceiving us.

Satan said to Jesus, *If You are the Son of God, command that these stones become bread* (Matthew 4:3). After forty days of fasting, it was natural for Jesus to want some bread. Wouldn't it have been a natural response for Him to say, "I have the right to make some bread. I am God and I am hungry"? Satan always sets you up in a position where it would seem okay to go ahead and flow with his lie. That's what happens when people compromise. "Don't I have the right to be happy?" Well, of course you do! "To be happy I am going to have to leave my spouse," or, "I am going to have to have sex before I am married," or, "I can't tithe this month." Satan sets us up to compromise Scripture and to go against the Word of God.

One argument of the secular world is, "Are you telling me that a woman who has been raped should bear the burden and carry the pain all of her life and make a child suffer for that terrible crime?"

"No, I wouldn't tell you that. I guess you'd better go ahead and kill the baby." See, it seems logical. "How could we be so terrible as to put the woman through that?"

We missed the whole point. How can we, as a society, get to the place where we kill our kids? Let's get back to reality instead of considering what seems and feels and sounds right. When we start reasoning with the devil, we get caught up in deception.

The devil says to Jesus, "If You are the Son of God, make bread." That sounds good. What is wrong with making bread after fasting for forty days and forty nights? Obviously, Jesus whipped the devil so why *would* He make bread? Only to prove that He is the Son of God. Why would He have to prove it? Because we don't believe what God said: **This is My beloved Son**. It all goes back to *questioning the Word*. Anytime you are lied to by the devil, in the end it gets back to questioning the Word.

Jesus said, **It is written, "Man shall not live by bread alone, but by every word that proceeds from the mouth of God"** (Matthew 4:4). What Word came from God? **This is My beloved Son, in whom I am well pleased** (Matthew 3:17). Jesus responded to Satan with the Word. We must have an understanding of the Word to keep ourselves free from Satan's lies. If you don't know the Word, you are susceptible to lies.

Renewal Truth

I am diligent to present myself approved unto God, a worker who needs not to be ashamed, rightly dividing the word of truth.
(2 Timothy 2:15)

How can someone who goes to church all their life be lied to and ripped off by the devil? People who have grown up in the church, faithful church members, deacons, and ushers, end up in adultery, fornication, poverty, disease, cancer, heart attacks, their kids pregnant, and their kids divorced. How can this happen to good Christian people? Although they went to church all their life, *they didn't get the Word.* All they got were three poems and a magazine article. They got a social gospel by a potbellied preacher who was trying to keep his job. They got some denominational mess, but they didn't get the Word. If there is no Word, you have nothing to live on because man lives by every word from God.

People need to be fed the Word of God, not philosophy, denominational doctrine, or a social gospel. People need the Word in them. If you don't get the Word, you are open prey to the lies of the devil.

Some people choose a church because they feel loved there. I've got news for you: Love isn't going to save you from the lies of the devil. People are getting ripped off, going through divorce, and they are literally going through hell, while they sit in "nice" churches. Some come to Christian Faith Center and say, "You are so serious." We are serious. There is a war going on, and if you don't get the Word in you, you are not going to make it.

Some people opt for a "nice" environment where they will end up with their kids out in the world, but they feel good about the "niceness"! That is a lie and a trick of the devil. We're not about "feeling nice." We are about making sure we have what it takes to live, and it takes a daily dose of God's Word to live.

Renewal Truth

Although grass withers and
flowers fade, the Word of God
stands forever.
(Isaiah 40:8)

Jesus was saying to the devil, "I don't have to respond to making bread, because I have the Word." Jesus did not buy into the temptation for food to prove who He was.

> *Then the devil took Him up into the holy city, set Him on the pinnacle of the temple, and said to Him, "If You are the Son of God, throw Yourself down. For it is written. . . ."*
>
> Matthew 4:5–6

The devil throws in a Scripture: *"He shall give His angels charge over you,"* and, *"In their hands they shall bear you up, lest you dash your foot against a stone"* (v. 6).

Satan perverts Scripture, and the average person who doesn't seek wise counsel will swallow it. Through perverting Scripture, he will make you feel justified to do the very thing that will destroy your life. Many people have quoted Scripture to me and then went off into sin.

Case in point: Satan tempts you with another woman—"You have the right to be happy. This woman would love you, care for you, and be a good wife. You need to lose your present wife and go get a new one." If you don't respond, Satan will bring Scripture: "Scripture says the woman is supposed to submit to the man. Your wife is not submitting to you, so you have a right to leave her. Paul said in 1 Corinthians, chapter 7, if she departs, let her depart." Now you have Scripture going around in your head to get you to sin.

People excuse and rationalize with Scripture. Jesus says, "No, I am not going to respond to you, Satan. I don't need bread to know who I am. I've got the Word of God."

Years ago I had a friend who traveled with me to Europe several times. He had a call of God on his life and was a great minister. He got in his head the crazy idea about leaving the church. "I don't need church. God is calling me to such and such." He quoted Scripture to me. A month later he was totally gone—drinking, smoking pot, and he left his wife and children. His life is history, and *he got there quoting Scripture.*

Many people tried to counsel him, "That's not what Scripture says." If you want to believe a lie, you can find a Scripture to back you up. This is where wise counsel and a multitude of counselors come in.

Jesus responded to Satan's lie, *It is written again, "You shall not tempt the Lord your God"* (v. 7). Then Satan tried another temptation for glory, power, and position. *Again, the devil took Him up on an exceedingly high mountain, showed Him all the kingdoms of the world and their glory. And he said to Him, "All these things I will give You if You will fall down and worship me"* (vv. 8–9).

Satan had the power to give it to Jesus because it had been given to him from Adam. Jesus responded, *Away with you, Satan! For it is written, "You shall worship the Lord your God, and Him only you shall serve"* (v. 10).

If you have a well-balanced perspective of Scripture, no matter what lie comes against you, you won't be tricked or deceived. Even Jesus, the Son of God, did not respond with what He thought at the moment. He responded with the logos—the written Word of God. He never said, "Well, I just don't feel good about this, Mr. Devil." He responded with, "It is written," followed by an exact quote of Scripture that was appropriate for each situation.

Major ministries that have fallen in the last few years weren't teaching the Word. They were emotional and promotional, great salesmen and media personalities, but they weren't Word based.

Back in the 50's, the *Voice of Healing* magazine was put out by a group of ministers. Many of them held their meetings in tents, and some competed to see who could get the biggest tent. Many of these men, anointed of God with outstanding miracles in their ministries, died young. The ones who died young weren't strong Word men, but they operated off of their gift.

When you are not strong with, "It is written," your life will not have long-term success.

Renewal Truth

Your Word is forever settled in heaven, Lord. It is a lamp to my feet and a light to my path.
(Psalm 119:89,105)

How are we to overcome the lies that bind? With the truth that frees, which is God's Word. If you will stay focused on the Word, you will have what it takes to say, "It is written," and not be tricked by the devil.

Personal Application of
Renewal Truths

1. To resist the devil, I must know God's Word. My knowledge of God's Word is growing by: _____

    _____

    _____

    _____

    _____

2. Satan's lies are exposed by: _____

    _____

    _____

    _____

    _____

3. Jesus gave me a "model" for dealing with Satan's lies. He handled the devil's lies by (see Matthew 4:1–11): _____

    _____

    _____

    _____

    _____

4. Does Satan's effectiveness come through power or through deception? Explain: _____

    _____

    _____

    _____

    _____

5. Satan has been stripped of authority. As a child of God, I can wipe out his power with the name of _____.

6

The Role of the Anointing in the Renewal Process

But you have an anointing from the Holy One, and you know all things.

1 John 2:20

As a young Christian, I did not understand this verse. There were many times when I knew things, yet I'd think, "How would I know? I'm young. Maybe I am wrong." As time went by, I found out that I was right. I knew something, either about an individual, about a ministry, or about something going on. Now that I look back, I realize the Holy Spirit anoints us *to know*.

In every area of life, we can trust God for an anointing to correspond with what He has called us to do. You can't disregard study or discipline, but you will have an anointing *to know* what you need to know to function in your life.

I trust God for the anointing to know how to be a husband, a father, and a pastor. 1 John 2:27 says: *But the anointing which you have received from Him abides in you.* This is true for all believers. The anointing doesn't come and go, it *abides.*

Now, one of the things that we have taught in our cruise-a-matic, charismatic world, is the Holy Spirit comes upon us, does His thing, leaves, and we go back out to the real world. We have a mentality that says we go into the anointing and then we come out of it. I am just as anointed at 7:00 Monday morning as I was at 11:00 a.m. on Sunday. The anointing abides in you.

If my little boy comes in at 8:00 on Friday night and says, "Dad, I've got a problem," I need the anointing of truth to help him, to teach him, and to minister to him. I can't say, "Let's just wait, son, and see if the Holy Ghost anoints us."

We need to get out of the "God is going to do something" mentality: "Here He comes." "When we all get to heaven." "In a little while." "When the revival hits." We need to get out of waiting for something from heaven and start recognizing the Holy Spirit has been poured out upon all flesh. He abides in us, and now as we are renewing our minds, we know truth and that truth is what is setting people free.

Renewal Truth

I shall decree what
should be—in line with
God's Word, which is His
will—and it shall be
established.
(Job 22:28 KJV)

The anointing lives and abides in us. We are not always sensitive to it or aware of it, but it is always there. He will never leave us or forsake us. Let me throw this one in for free: Most of the time what we consider "the anointing" in a service is simply getting our faith turned on and getting excited about what God can do. It is more of an emotional thing in our lives than a change in the spirit world, not that the Holy Ghost doesn't come in and do unique things at times.

1 John 2:27 goes on: *And you do not need that anyone teach you* [this means that you know what is right and how the Holy Spirit is leading, because you have an anointing that abides in you]; *but as the same anointing teaches you concerning all things, and is true, and is not a lie, and just as it has taught you, you will abide in Him.*

The Holy Spirit leads us into all truth, not into lies. What about the preacher who says, "You don't need to pray in tongues. Just do what we tell you to do. We will tell you what is right. Our doctrine . . . our headquarters . . . our denomination . . . we know all truth."

In such cases, we have done away with the need for a personal relationship with Jesus Christ and we have just become another religious group. We have to be careful that we do not start relying on 24-hour-a-day Christian television to have other people answer all of our questions. If Christian television, your pastor, your home group leader, your mentor, and everybody else could answer every question, then why would you need the Holy Ghost? Each of us needs a personal relationship with God.

Usually when you ask other people a question, you already know the answer. You are just trying to find someone to confirm what you believe, or you are looking for a way out of what you know you are supposed to do. Because the anointing abides in you, you know the truth.

How come more people aren't sensitive to the Spirit? Their minds aren't renewed to the Word, so they get confused or have so many goofy thoughts. If you could put the average person's brain on a video screen, it would scare you! You would have Halloween right in front of your face, because the average person is so caught up in the thoughts and attitudes of the world that, though they love God, they have not been transformed to believe, think, and act like God believes, thinks, and acts.

Renewal Truth

I am being transformed
continually by the renewing
of my mind with God's Word,
that I may know the good,
acceptable, and perfect will
of God.
(Romans 12:2)

I believe to love God with all your heart, soul, and mind means to have your soul plugged in, loving God with your mind, emotions, and will. I want you to really understand this, when I say "heart and soul," that I mean "with all your mind." That means you are going to have to change every thought that is contrary to loving God.

In raising my children, if they have attitudes that do not reveal a love for God, I have to help them get plugged in to the Word and get their thoughts changed. It is natural for us to have negative attitudes. The world and the flesh are negative. So if you are not loving God with all your heart, soul, and mind, then you are going to have all kinds of problems. You won't be able to flow in the anointing that will lead you into all truth. Your mind is set on lies, compromises, attitudes, fears, worries, and negative things so what you are feeling inside isn't registering because your mind isn't sensitive to it.

When people listen to a song, all some hear are the words, while others hear the instruments. The one tuning the piano has his ear tuned to the right tone and he can hear a variation in tone that you or I might not hear. He plays the notes and says, "It's out of key," when we might say, "It sounded good to me." His ear is trained.

My friend, Terry Tarsiuk, and I were listening to a CD in my car. He said, "Man, I love the instrumental," and started naming weird instruments I'd never even heard of. I thought, "I didn't hear that, but did you catch that drum line?" While I am sensitive to drums because that is what I play, he is sensitive to the other instruments because that is what he is into. Whatever you train your ear to hear, that is what you will hear.

While sitting in a room with a group of people, suddenly a mother says, "My baby is crying." You say, "I didn't hear anything." Her ear is tuned to her child. Most mothers can even determine the difference in the "kind" of cry, whether it's a "hungry" cry, a "change me" cry, or a "hold me" cry.

• The same thing happens in the Christian walk. When your mind is renewed to the truth, your ear is dialed to the anointing, because the anointing leads you into all truth. Your ear is tuned to truth because you have renewed your mind to truth. As the anointing begins to flow, you know what God is doing and you know His will. But if your brain is like scrambled eggs, void of the anointing, you are thinking, "I don't know. I don't understand. I am scared. What is going to happen?" You will talk like the average Christian.

John said, *Beloved, I pray that you may prosper in all things and be in health, just as your soul prospers* (3 John 2). A "prosperous soul" is one that *testifies* of the truth that is in them and causes them to walk in truth.

> *For I rejoiced greatly when brethren came and testified of the truth that is in you, just as you walk in the truth. I have no greater joy than to hear that my children walk in truth.*
>
> 3 John 3–4

A prosperous soul abides in the truth of God's Word, and the Spirit of truth leads and guides them into all truth because they are sensitive to it.

The anointing that leads and guides them into all truth flows freely so they are prospering in their soul. They are plugged into the truth, both through the Word and through the anointing. Now they have health and prosperity in every area of life. It works. But if you reject truth and don't have time for truth, the Spirit of truth can't work and the anointing can't flow. Everything gets jammed up, and you will have problems in your life. Your soul prospers, depending on the level of truth that is operating in your life.

PAUL PRAYS TRUTH UPON THE CHURCH AT EPHESUS

In Ephesians, chapter 1, Paul is praying for the church at Ephesus, and what is good for the church at Ephesus is good for us. He says (verse 15):

> *After I heard of your faith in the Lord Jesus and your love for all the saints, (I) do not cease to give thanks for you, making men-*

88

tion of you in my prayers: That the God of our Lord Jesus Christ,
the Father of glory, may give to you the spirit of wisdom and
revelation in the knowledge of Him.

Ephesians 1:15–17

"The spirit of wisdom and revelation in the knowledge of God"
refers to the Spirit of truth. The Spirit of truth brings wisdom (how
to apply the truth) and revelation (a revealing of the truth) of the
knowledge of God. Paul is praying that the work of the Holy Spirit
will happen in this young church's life because he knows that their
success, victory, and prosperity as Christians are dependent upon
their walk in truth. It is not dependent on how many miracles they
have seen.

Renewal Truth

Because God's power (His
Spirit) is at work in me, He
is able to do exceedingly
abundantly above all that I
could ever ask or think.
(Ephesians 3:20)

Wisdom is to know truth and to know how to apply it. How do
we know when a person is wise? They do things that work and
that bring good results.

A woman may know about proper relationships with men and
about guarding and protecting her life, but that doesn't mean she

89

is a wise woman. But when a woman doesn't get involved with carnal men, or become trapped in her emotions and desires for improper relationships, and doesn't find herself being used and abused by men of the world, then we would say, "This is a wise woman." It is in her application of truth that we see wisdom.

PRAYING FOR OTHERS

How can we pray for people in our churches and families to help them be the people God wants them to be? To help them find success in their lives?

In Ephesians 1:17, when Paul speaks of the Spirit of wisdom, he is speaking of the *Spirit of God*—not some angelic spirit, a human spirit, or a demonic spirit. It is the Spirit of God who brings wisdom and revelation in the knowledge of God.

When we pray for people, we pray that they will be healed. We pray that people will prosper. We pray that they will have success in life. But notice, when Paul prays for them, he prays that they will *know the right things.* That is the key for them to be healed, prospered, and to have success in life. When John prays for them in 3 John 2, he prays that they will prosper, *even as their soul prospers,* because he knows that is the key to their success in life.

Far too often, we pray for a change of the *symptoms* rather than a change of the root cause of the problem. We want the body healed, but we fail to go after the thing that caused the sickness in the first place. We want the checking account to be prosperous, but we fail to identify what made us poor in the first place. If we go after the Spirit of wisdom and revelation in the knowledge of God, then healing, prosperity, and success will come. Why? Because now we are abiding in the anointing and the anointing is leading and guiding us into all truth. And when you know the truth, you will prosper in all things.

Renewal Truth

Because I abide in Jesus
and His Word abides in me,
whatever I ask in line with
His will, He does for me.
(John 15:7)

Paul goes on in Ephesians 1:18 to say: *The eyes of your understanding being enlightened; that you may know.* Paul is praying for us to know something. He is praying for us to have revelation and wisdom in the knowledge of God. So we can know *the hope of His calling, what are the riches of the glory of His inheritance in the saints, and what is the exceeding greatness of His power toward us who believe, according to the working of His mighty power which He worked in Christ when He raised Him from the dead* (v. 18–20).

Why doesn't Paul just say, "I pray that the power will hit you upside the head"? If you don't understand how to walk in truth and power, what it really means is, once a church service is over you will go back out into the real world facing the same problems, and you will end up in the same negative circumstances again. We have tried to impart the power, but we didn't pray that they would *know the power.* Paul prays that we would *know.* Then, no matter where we are, whether the preacher is present or not, whether it is Sunday or not, whether we have our friend beside us or not, if we have the Spirit of wisdom and revelation, we will be led by the truth (God's Word).

Usually, we pray for the power to come down, but Paul prayed for us to know what Jesus has already done for us. It seems to me that we are always trying to get God to do something, and Paul is praying that *we would plug into what He has already done.*

```
┌─────────────────────────────────────┐
│                                     │
│          Renewal Truth              │
│                                     │
│      The Lord has done great        │
│          things for me.             │
│          (Psalm 126:2)              │
│                                     │
└─────────────────────────────────────┘
```

Paul prayed that we would know *what is the greatness of His power toward us who believe, according to the working of His mighty power which He worked in Christ when He raised Him from the dead and seated Him at His right hand in the heavenly places* (Ephesians 1:19–20).

That resurrection power is now ours. While we pray, "God, send a revival," God is saying, "I sent My Son, I have poured out My Spirit, I have given you My Word, and I have sent laborers to help you understand it, and you are still waiting for something to happen. What else can I do?"

I remember sitting in a Bible school some twenty years ago. One of my teachers was talking about the days of revival in 1948, and he said, "Those days are coming back and they are going to hit us anytime." He believed revival was to hit before the 90's. I raised my hand and asked, "Do we just have to wait for it, or is there something we can do to kick start it?" He said we had to wait on God's timing. I went out and started a church which grew to four or five times the size of his church within two years. We went ahead and had our revival, and he is still waiting on revival!

This mentality needs to be replaced with the knowledge of what God has already done for us. This is what the renewal of the mind is all about. I am not waiting on God—He is waiting on me. As I am transformed by the renewing of my mind, I begin to establish the perfect will of God. I think when Jesus told the disciples how to pray, He was giving them the perspective that we must have. *In this manner, therefore, pray: Our Father in heaven, hallowed be Your name. Your kingdom come* (Matthew 6:9–10).

That wasn't a question or a request. It was a *demand* on what God has given. "Thy Kingdom be established," not "Thy Kingdom, I'm coming." *Thy kingdom come.* Establish it. Make it happen. Put it into the lives of people on earth. Then *Your will be done*, not, "If it be Thy will."

Know the will of God and establish it. *Your will be done on earth as it is in heaven* (v. 10). Not, "I can't wait to get to heaven." No, *Your will be done on earth*, not "I can't wait until I'm out of here, man. I've got the Jonah spirit on me." If you've got Jonah's attitude, God will find you a special prayer room (like the belly of a whale) and it won't be comfy!

This attitude that Jesus is giving us is not, "The Kingdom of God is coming." His Kingdom is in us. We are to establish it and demand that the will of God be done in the earth now. I am helping people to receive this truth and establish it in their own lives. I'm not just waiting for something to hit. It has already hit! Jesus gave His life, the Holy Spirit has come, the truth has been given. Now, go on and make it happen in your life.

Personal Application of
Renewal Truths

1. I am tuning my ears to hear truth by: _____
    _____
    _____
    _____
    _____

2. *Wisdom* is: _____
    _____

3. *Revelation* is: _____
    _____

4. My soul is prospering because: _____
    _____
    _____
    _____

5. The result of prosperity in my mind is: _____
    _____
    _____
    _____

7

The Role of the Human Will in the Renewal Process

Seek the Lord while He may be found, call upon Him while He is near.

Isaiah 55:6

This Scripture implies that there will come a day when the Lord will not be found. Then verse 7 goes on to say:

Let the wicked forsake his way, and the unrighteous man his thoughts; let him return to the Lord, and He will have mercy on him; and to our God, for He will abundantly pardon.

•Part of the process of seeking the Lord is to forsake thoughts that do not come from righteousness. We are to renew our thoughts with God's Word to agree with what God says. In reality, you do not *return to the Lord* until you begin to forsake your own thoughts and change your thinking to agree with God's thoughts.

Isaiah 55, verses 8 and 9, say:

"For My thoughts are not your thoughts, nor are your ways My ways," says the Lord. "For as the heavens are higher than the earth, so are My ways higher than your ways, and My thoughts than your thoughts."

The Lord spoke to me years ago about this passage of Scripture. He said, "When you have My thoughts, you have My ways. If you don't have My thoughts, you don't have My ways."

If we want God's ways for our children, we need His thoughts about being a parent. If we want God's ways, His blessing and His provision in our business, we must have His ways in our mind. When we have God's thoughts, we will have His ways.

When I go into a situation, I ask, "Lord, what are You thinking about this?" Because if I am thinking what God is thinking, I can figure out how He is going to move. When I have His thoughts, I can have His ways.

Scripture says, *He* [God] *made known His ways to Moses, His acts to the children of Israel* (Psalm 103:7). In other words, Moses knew more about God than just the miracles that He did. The people didn't want to know. They didn't plug in. Remember, the people said to Moses, "Don't let God talk to us. You talk to God and tell us what He says." They didn't want to hear God's thoughts, so they didn't know His ways.

You have to decide what kind of Christian you want to be. Do you want to see the acts of God occasionally, or are you going to be one who presses in to know His thoughts so you can know His ways? A successful Christian moves in God's ways because he (or she) knows God's thoughts.

Renewal Truth

Because I know God's thoughts
and His ways through the Holy
Spirit, I am strong and I am
doing great exploits to bring
glory to Him.
(Daniel 11:32)

Paul said, *But the natural man does not receive the things of the Spirit of God, for they are foolishness to him; nor can he know them, because they are spiritually discerned* (1 Corinthians 2:14).

The natural man cannot get hold of the thoughts of God. If you think like the average guy in the world, you will never understand what God is thinking, because to know the thoughts of God, you have to think spiritually. His thoughts are spiritually discerned.

When you think in line with the Word, which is truth, you are spiritually minded and spiritually discerning. You will begin to hear, understand, and perceive the thoughts of God.

> *But he who is spiritual judges all things, yet he himself is rightly judged by no one. For "who has known the mind of the Lord that he may instruct Him?" But we have the mind of Christ.*
> 1 Corinthians 2:15–16

As we become sensitive to the Spirit of God and become spiritually minded, we will begin to possess the mind of Christ. Our natural, carnal thoughts will be replaced with God's thoughts.

Perhaps you are a young man who is looking for a wife. You begin a relationship with a girl and you question, "Is this the right girl?" If you are spiritually minded, God's anointing will lead you and you will know. The anointing that abides in you will teach you all truth. If you are not thinking with your hormones, with your physical desires like the average guy in the world, you will know whether the girl is right or not. You won't have to go to fourteen counselors and twelve pastors and take a personality test. You will know.

A problem develops when your hormones are stronger than the mind of Christ in your life. You are thinking, "But she's got the right hair and she goes to church." She is as carnal as the dog down the street, but she goes to church and she is pretty.

You can't hear the anointing. You can't hear the mind of Christ. On the inside of you, the anointing is trying to lead you into all truth, saying, "No, no, no! This is *not* the woman that will help you fulfill your destiny."

Renewal Truth

The fruit of the Holy Spirit —
love, joy, peace, longsuffering,
kindness, goodness, faithfulness,
gentleness, and self-control—are
maturing in my human spirit.
(Galatians 5:22–23)

You are trying to get what your natural man wants, and the natural man does not hear or receive the things of the Spirit of

God because the things of the Spirit are spiritually discerned. You are not spiritually discerning, so you are missing the mind of Christ. Therefore, you don't have the thoughts or the ways of God.

Six months down the road you go to your pastor seeking counsel, either because you have gotten into a worldly relationship and you have ended up in sin, or you are hurt, let down, and discouraged. You say, "I don't understand how this could happen to me." It happened because you didn't forsake your own thoughts and plug into God's thoughts so you could have His way in your relationship.

• Each day we should seek for the higher thoughts (God's thoughts) and the higher ways of thinking. If we will do that, then we will begin to have God's way in our relationships, in our finances, in our ministry or careers, and in everything we do. Every day we are faced with a choice: Do I think the thoughts of the natural man, or do I think the thoughts of God?

The human soul is made up of the mind, will, and emotions. The things of the Spirit are eternal, and we are supernaturally affected when we are born of God. The things of the soul are naturally and gradually affected as we grow, learn, and renew the mind with the Word of God. So the will of a person must be renewed as part of the process of renewing the mind.

Paul prayed, *Now may the God of peace Himself sanctify you completely; and may your whole spirit, soul, and body be preserved blameless at the coming of our Lord Jesus Christ* (1 Thessalonians 5:23). The "will" is part of the soul realm, and it must be renewed and developed.

The human will is almost like a muscle. When you practice anything with your physical muscles, they learn to do things better. Soon they will do things automatically. So it is with the human will. Whatever you do over and over will begin to become automatic.

GOD GAVE MAN THE ABILITY TO "CHOOSE"

We are going to look at the will and see how it works in the negative world and in the positive world, and how we need to use our will as we develop our spiritual mind.

Let's go back to the book of beginnings, the book of Genesis. In chapter 1 God created the heavens and the earth, plants and animal life. He spoke the creation process into being. But when He came to man, He said, *Let Us make man in Our image, according to Our likeness* (Genesis 1:26). Something took place in the creation process that hadn't happened before. God had been creating out of His mind, out of His infinite wisdom, and out of His infinite ability. But now He says, "We are going to create something that is like Us."

> *"Let them [man] have dominion over the fish of the sea, over the birds of the air, and over the cattle, over all the earth and over every creeping thing that creeps on the earth." So God created man in His own image; in the image of God He created him; male and female He created them. Then God blessed them, and God said to them, "Be fruitful and multiply; fill the earth and subdue it; have dominion."*
>
> Genesis 1:26–28

When God created Adam and Eve in His likeness and image, He gave them dominion and authority and sent them out to possess and subdue the earth. He put something in them that was not in any animal or plant. He put something in them that was unique, as we read earlier in the book, and that is *the ability to choose*, or the will.

Throughout his lifetime, man makes decisions about what he is going to do and why he is going to do it. Humans ask questions, such as, "Do I like myself?" Humans get depressed and call up a friend and say, "I hate my life."

Humans look at other humans and say, "Hey, wait a minute. I want to be like Mike." Or, "I want something different in my life." It might motivate you to get an education and do other things, or it may just frustrate you as you sit in your sense of victimization. But man has a will and he is aware of it. What you do with it is dependent upon how you train and develop that muscle.

•Part of being created in the likeness and image of God—this divine gifting of the human being—is you get to make choices. We read in Isaiah 55:8, *For My thoughts are not your thoughts. You can choose to forsake your thoughts, take God's thoughts and live on a higher level, with a new way of life.*

Many people don't think they can change their way of life. Some feel trapped by circumstances and what they have been told: "You are a victim." "You are white." "You are black." And on and on. . . .

Some people will choose to fight with the union to see if they can get an extra quarter an hour. They struggle with some dumb thing to see if they can improve their existence to some degree, but they don't believe that they can have a different way of living. When you grasp the fact that you can have whatever way of life you choose, then you will become a self-empowered, self-motivated individual.

A few hundred years ago, a group of people said, "We don't have to live under the bondage of a monarchy or a controlling religious system that is wicked and evil. We can choose another way of life." They packed up their goods and headed out of town, and went to a new world to make a new life because they recognized the power of their will. That has not changed. There may not be new lands for you to discover, but there is some place where you can go to do whatever you want to do, good, bad, or indifferent. You have a will, and depending on how you use it, you can have whatever way of life you want.

If you choose God's thoughts, you will get God's ways, and that is the highest level of life. That is what I am seeking after. I don't want my way. I want His way. Jesus said in Matthew 10:39 AMP: *Whoever finds his [lower] life will lose it [the higher life], and whoever loses his [lower] life on My account will find it [the higher life].*

If you give up your way of thinking and take His way of thinking, you will find a higher level of life. This is true for your marriage, for your children, your finances, your ministry or career, and for everything that you do.

God gave Adam and Eve a will and asked them to use it wisely. If they had obeyed God, they could have lived the high life. As we discussed earlier, it was the devil's deception, *not his power*, that tripped up Adam and Eve. Neither is it Satan's power that is affecting Christians today. It is his deception, lies, trickery, subtleties, and cunning ways. When Adam and Eve began to think the thoughts of the devil, they lost their relationship with God. By a "choice" of their will, they were separated from Him.

What kind of existence do you want? Life or death, blessing or cursing, positive or negative, joy or depression, prosperity or poverty, sickness or health? It is your choice. I am convinced that the average person just feels like they are caught up in a whirlwind, they are being carried along, and they really can't help it or change anything. But the fact is, *you can make a choice to live a higher level of life in Christ.*

Let's assume a little boy is raised up in a poor part of town. His dad and mom are just trying to keep the bills paid. He is confronted with drugs and sex and crime every day of his life. Although he is under some terrific negative influences, *he still has a choice* to make as to whether he will be a part of it or not.

Another case in point: I know several ministers who were raised in drugs, sickness, poverty, and sin, but today they are preaching the Gospel. One such man is Eric Morrison. At seven years of age, he watched as his mom was shot to death in a dope deal. Today he is preaching the Gospel. His first seven years of life were with a single parent in the midst of the worst kind of sin and degradation. At seven, with no parent, he tried to survive. As a young man he sought the Lord, changed his choices, was born of God, and is now a minister. He is affecting thousands of lives around his community, his church, and the nation through his teaching and his witness. To me, this is proof that *life is a choice.*

He could have stayed where he was and said, "I can't help it. My mamma was shot when I was seven. I was raised in sin and crime. What do you expect?" I expect you to choose to get out! "I can't help it." Yes, you can, because *you are created in the likeness and image of God.* He has set before you life and death, blessing and cursing. *You* choose which one you are going to have. Every person has this choice.

AN INFUSION OF HOPE IN MY LIFE

I was raised without a knowledge of God. I believed in God, but I had no knowledge of God or His Word. At thirteen years of age, I was drinking, smoking pot, and using drugs. I was trying to have fun. I figured life existed so I could get high, have fun, and if I died high, then I would die good!

By the time I was nineteen, I was burned out because it doesn't work. It was not producing the kind of life I wanted. I ended up in jail and was all messed up with drugs, crime, problems, and depression. I was confronted with life and death, blessing and cursing. A man said to me, "You can continue to be the way you are, or you can choose something different." I chose, **Whoever calls on the name of the Lord shall be saved** (Romans 10:13).

How You Live Is *Your* Choice

The divine gift of choosing how you will live can be buried in such thoughts as:

- I am a victim.
- I can't help it.
- It's my circumstances.
- It's my age.
- It's my race.

Under all of these lies is a divine gift that makes you like God with a will to choose life or death, blessing or cursing, poverty or prosperity, sickness or health. You have the privilege of making a choice.

The secular world tries to escape the reality that man has a will. They blame genetics, the environment, or the government. The truth is, each of us is who we are because of our choices.

You are not a lesbian because of lesbian hormones or genetics. You are a lesbian because you chose to reject the godly way and pervert the desires of the flesh. You are not a homosexual because of your hormones, your genetics, or anything else. You are a homosexual by your own choice.

If we were to turn back your life, we would find where relationships with others have affected and influenced you in such a way that your choices have caused you to become perverted. That doesn't mean you are a wicked, evil, negative person. It just means you made choices to end up in a very dangerous lifestyle.

You are not a heroin addict because of genetics or hormones. You are a heroin addict because of your choices. You are not an alcoholic because of your hormones, genetics, or anything else. You are an alcoholic by choice. You may think some people become alcoholics easier than others, but that doesn't take away the choice you made to follow that lifestyle. Some people gain weight easier than others, but we still make choices in diet and exercise.

Your "will" affects every area of life. Joshua said:

> *And if it seems evil to you to serve the Lord, choose for your-selves this day whom you will serve, whether the gods which your fathers served that were on the other side of the River, or the gods of the Amorites, in whose land you dwell. But as for me and my house, we will serve the Lord.*
>
> Joshua 24:15

In modern society, we want to say, "Well, I hope everything works out okay based on genetics and the environmental influence." Joshua says, *it is your choice.* Our lives reveal our choices.

MARY MADE A CHOICE

Remember when Jesus went into a certain village and paid a visit to the home of Mary and Martha? While Mary made a choice to sit at Jesus' feet and hear the Word, Martha was caught up in natural preparations. Let's read this account in Luke 10:38–41:

> *Now it happened as they went that He entered a certain village; and a certain woman named Martha welcomed Him into her house. And she had a sister called Mary, who also sat at Jesus' feet and heard His word. But Martha was distracted with much serving, and she approached Him and said, "Lord, do You not care that my sister has left me to serve alone? Therefore tell her to help me." And Jesus answered and said to her, "Martha, Martha."*

When the Lord says any word twice, you are in trouble! *"Martha, Martha, you are worried and troubled about many things"* (v. 41).

Martha said, "My problem is, Mary won't help me." Jesus says, "No, that is not your problem. You have a whole bunch of problems. You have piled up things in your life that have distracted, depressed, and worried you. Mary is *not* your problem. You are troubled about many things." Then Jesus says, **But one thing is needed, and Mary has chosen that good part, which will not be taken away from her** (v. 42).

Here is a microcosm of human will in operation. Mary chose to sit at Jesus' feet and hear His Word. Martha chose many thoughts, attitudes, and behaviors that were troubling her. She complains about the condition of her life, and Jesus says, "Mary made a choice, and it is not going to be taken away from her." In other words, "Now Martha, it is time for you to make a choice and deal with those things that are troubling your life."

Renewal Truth

My first priority in life
is to seek God's Kingdom and
His righteousness.
(Matthew 6:33)

Complaining to God about your life won't change anything. That's why a lot of people pray negative, whiny, complaining prayers, and wonder why nothing happens. What did you ask for? "I told God how I felt. I told Him I didn't need anyone. Doesn't He understand?" God answered your prayer. He just nodded His head at how miserable you are. Whining and complaining to God won't change a thing. You have chosen to be the way you are and where you are. When you start saying, "Lord, I am going to make some new choices," God says, "Now I can get involved."

- "Lord, I believe I am healed in the name of Jesus." Jesus responds, "I can confirm that" (1 Peter 2:24; Isaiah 53:5).
- "Lord, I am prospering and getting out of debt." God says, "I can get involved in that" (Joshua 1:8; Psalm 1:1–3).
- "The joy of the Lord is my strength. No more depression for me!" The Lord responds, "I can confirm that" (Nehemiah 8:10; Isaiah 54:14,17).

Now God has something to work with because you are starting to change and make godly choices. As long as you are just complaining about your circumstances, the Lord says the same thing to you as He said to Martha. "Lord, I am having a bad day. Don't You know how my boss treats me?" The Lord says, "Martha, Martha, it's not only your boss, you have many things that you are troubled about." ***Mary has chosen.*** She made a choice. Mary is sitting at Jesus' feet, hearing the Word, and Martha is worried and troubled, all because of *choices.*

PAUL'S CHOICE

For to me, to live is Christ, and to die is gain. But if I live on in the flesh, this will mean fruit from my labor; yet what I shall choose I cannot tell.

Philippians 1:21–22

Paul says, "To live is okay, but to die in Christ is better. I am going to have to choose. If I stay and continue to preach, teach, and minister, it will produce fruit for the Kingdom and for your life."

What I shall choose I cannot tell. For I am hard-pressed between the two, having a desire to depart and be with Christ, which is far better. Nevertheless to remain in the flesh is more needful for you.

Philippians 1:22–24

Think of it. Here is a guy who is so developed in his relationship with God and, in control of his own will, he says, "Man, I would like to go and be with the Lord right now."

In 2 Timothy 4:7, Paul says, *I have fought the good fight, I have finished the race, I have kept the faith.* In other words, "I have done what the Lord has asked me to do." So now he is saying to the Philippians, "I would be better off to go be with Jesus. It is a whole lot better than hanging around here. But to stay and minister, teach, and preach would be good for you."

And being confident of this, I know that I shall remain and continue with you for your progress and joy of faith.

Philippians 1:25

Paul is writing, "I have made up my mind I am going to stay and keep ministering for your joy in the faith." In other words, "I will remain." He made a choice, an act of his will.

Again, the New Testament pattern is not, "Come quickly, Lord Jesus. Let me out of here. Where is the rapture bus?" The New Testament pattern is, "I am choosing that which is right for God's will and work in my life, and for those that I will influence."

It's time to quit waiting on the rapture bus and get on with what God wants you to do with your life.

Personal Application of
Renewal Truths

1. Unlike animals who live by instinct, I live by: _____
   _____
   _____

2. The highest level of life for me is: _____
   _____
   _____
   _____

3. I can achieve a higher level of life by: _____
   _____
   _____
   _____
   _____
   _____

4. Some of the challenges I am facing right now, along with the Scriptures I am using to make godly choices in each situation, are:

Challenge	*Scripture*
_____	_____
_____	_____
_____	_____
_____	_____
_____	_____
_____	_____

5. Like Paul, it is my desire to be a "servant" to others by:

_____

_____

_____

_____

_____

_____

To order additional copies please call:

1-800-644-4446

or write to

P.O. Box 98800
Seattle, WA 98198